THE
ITALIAN
COOKBOOK

THE ITALIAN COOKBOOK

The best of Italian food

Consultant Editor
Fiona Biggs

Bath · New York · Singapore · Hong Kong · Cologne · Delhi
Melbourne · Amsterdam · Johannesburg · Auckland · Shenzhen

This edition published by Parragon in 2011

Parragon Publishing
Queen Street House
4 Queen Street
Bath BA1 1HE, UK
www.parragon.com

ISBN: 978-1-4454-4893-0

Printed in China

Produced by terryjeavons&company

Notes for the Reader
This book uses imperial, metric, and US cup measurements. Follow the same
units of measurement throughout; do not mix imperial and metric. All spoon
measurements are level: teaspoons are assumed to be 5 ml, and tablespoons
are assumed to be 15 ml. Unless otherwise stated, milk is assumed to be
whole, eggs and individual vegetables such as potatoes are medium, and
pepper is freshly ground black pepper.

The times given are an approximate guide only. Preparation times differ
according to the techniques used by different people and the cooking times
may also vary from those given as a result of the type of oven used. Optional
ingredients, variations or serving suggestions have not been included in the
calculations.

Recipes using raw or very lightly cooked eggs should be avoided by infants, the
elderly, pregnant women, convalescents, and anyone with a chronic condition.
Pregnant and breastfeeding women are advised to avoid eating peanuts and
peanut products. Sufferers from nut allergies should be aware that some of the
ready-prepared ingredients used in the recipes in this book may contain nuts.
Always check the packaging before use.

Picture Acknowledgements
The publisher would like to thank the following for permission to reproduce
copyright material on the front cover: Close up of basil leaves © Tom
Merton/Getty Images, Spaghetti pasta strands © Creative Crop/Getty Images
and Delicious tomatoes filling vertical frame © Rosemary Calvert/Getty Images

contents

introduction

This book is a comprehensive guide to choosing, preparing and cooking Italian food. Lovers of Italian food will be pleased to find their favourite, classic dishes in addition to a number of new, imaginative recipes in one volume.

The front of the book is packed with information on Italy's favourite ingredients, essential tips for making and cooking perfect pasta and risotto and kitchen equipment that will make food preparation easier; along with all the basic recipes. The inspiring collection of recipes that follows caters for every occasion.

Bursting with freshness, colour and flavour, this book will make your mouth water. With such a choice of recipes you'll wonder where to begin. Perhaps the answer is, at the beginning as the Italians do, with a little antipasto to tempt the tastebuds!

the italian way

We may think of Italy as having a national cuisine but, apart from the pasta and pizza that can be found everywhere, there are strong differences from region to region between the top of its boot to the toe. As the climate and terrain change, so too does the cuisine, which reflects the enormous variety of local produce, specialities, traditions and economy of each of the regions.

It wasn't until the Unification of Italy in 1861 that each of the individual states, with their own identity, customs and cuisine, were combined as a single political entity – the Italy that we know today. Over the years, the borders have become more blurred as people have moved around the country, taking their specialities with them, but it is still almost impossible to define Italian cuisine.

Italian cooking was first inspired by the ancient Romans and then influenced by Greek, Byzantine and Arab invaders. Other influences were Italy's proximity to France and Austria and the produce brought to the country by the traders who sailed the seas. Venice, once the heart of the world's trading empire, was where ships brought cargoes of lemons and oranges from Asia, spinach from Persia, spices from Syria and Turkey and aubergines from South-East Asia, not forgetting tomatoes from Peru.

In each of Italy's distinctively regional cuisines the local produce is shown great respect. To the Italians, quality and freshness are very important. They learn about food from a very early age – mothers pass down recipes to daughters – centuries-old recipes are still being used and families

guard their recipes jealously. It is wonderful how they have managed to retain their traditions despite the hectic world in which we now live. They enjoy their food and have the ability to turn a simple family meal into a special occasion.

Although these days most products are available all year round and seasonal produce is not an issue, to the Italian cook the seasons are still of the utmost importance. The Italians take great pride in choosing their ingredients and treat their food with respect. There are fruit and vegetable markets in all Italian towns and Italian cooks will not necessarily go there to buy what they have decided to cook that day, but to choose what is fresh and in season—plump figs, juicy oranges, black and white grapes, ripe cherries, small courgettes with their orange flowers intact, and tiny sweet tomatoes still attached to the vine.

The same principle applies at the fish market – the Italian cook will select plump, bright whole fish, prawns still wriggling in their shells, everything freshly caught that morning. Since most of the regions of Italy are bordered by sea and there are many freshwater rivers and lakes in the north, there is an abundance of fish, and it is hardly surprising that the Italians are enthusiastic fish eaters. Local fish markets can be found in most towns and who, on a visit to Venice, hasn't visited La Madonna, the bustling fish market near the Rialto Bridge? The sheer beauty of the fish, trays and trays of different shapes and colours, is a sight for sore eyes.

In the colder north, food is richer and heartier. Cows are bred on fresh grass and provide not only beef and veal but also excellent dairy produce, such as butter and Parmesan cheese. There is even a recipe from the north of Italy for beef braised in milk! Many families raise a pig, feeding it on the whey left over from cheesemaking and hence pork, bacon, sausages, salami and ham are widely eaten. In addition, during the hunting season, game is often on the menu. The north is where rice is grown and is evident in the eating of risotto, and, more importantly, it is also where maize is grown and polenta is eaten.

In fact polenta is a staple diet in northern Italy and Italians from the south refer to northerners as 'polentoni' (polenta eaters). Apples are produced on a large scale, together with vegetables such as potatoes, swedes, cabbages, cauliflowers, celery, artichokes, asparagus and beans. In Tuscany the latter are eaten in such large

quantities, in every way imaginable, that the people are known as 'Toscani Mangiafagioli' (The Tuscan Bean-Eaters). Wild mushrooms and truffles are collected in the autumn in the beech and oak woods that are to be found throughout northern and central Italy and are highly sought after – hunters are even required to be licensed. Chicken and lamb are popular in Tuscany, as is calf's liver. The region of Venice is also is famous for its calf's liver, where the liver of calves under a year old is served fried and smothered with onions ('fegato alla Veneziana').

Shredded Spinach & Ham Risotto: Rice is a staple ingredient in the Italian diet and risotti are frequently served.

Although the region of Liguria is in the north, on the west coast, the Mediterranean climate is perfect for the production of garlic, basil and pine kernels. The coast is also full of olive groves and the oil produced is mild and sweet and considered by many to be the best. It is this oil that is used to make one of north-western Piedmont's most famous dishes, a hot dip known as Bagna Cauda. This is served in a pot, over a burner, and makes an ideal first course or light meal. It is made by heating 150 ml/5 fl oz olive oil, 85 g/3 oz butter and 2 chopped garlic cloves in a pan for 2 minutes, adding two 50 g/1¾ oz cans of drained and finely chopped anchovies and heating gently for 10 minutes, stirring all the time. The dip is served with sticks of raw vegetables such as celery, carrots, asparagus and courgettes, and crusty bread, which are dipped into it.

Moving southwards towards central Italy, the fertile land produces broccoli and fennel, as well as salad vegetables and herbs. The mountainous area of central Italy is a region of sheep farmers, and lamb, cooked in a variety of ways, is usually the main course. Mountain game such as wild boar can be found slightly further south.

Lamb Shanks with Roasted Onions: Slow-roasting lamb brings out its flavour and cuts from older animals also benefit from slow cooking techniques.

When we reach southern Italy the weather is warmer and this is the area of lighter food. Colourful fruits, such as oranges and lemons, and vegetables, including ripe tomatoes, peppers, courgettes, artichokes and aubergines, feature strongly, as does the colourful pizza. Pizzas are made throughout the country but it is said that the best are made in Naples and southern Italy. It was the Neapolitans who first used the tomato, brought to Italy by sailors from South America in the sixteenth century, when it was known as the evil golden apple of Eden as it was eaten while still green. The southern Italians let it ripen and turn red in their hot sun before eating. Now it is still their most valued product and is eaten fresh, used in cooked dishes and sauces, canned, puréed and dried.

Then there are Italy's islands. At the tip of the toe is Sicily, where the cooking is based on rice, couscous, vegetables, fish and citrus fruits, particularly lemons, which, along with almond trees, grow in great quantity. Sardinia, off Italy's west coast, is where lamb, pork, game, vegetables and cheese play the key role. Sardinians also have a wide range of bread and cakes, which often contain almonds and citrus fruits.

Seafood Pizza: Bags of fresh mixed seafood, containing prawns, squid rings, mussels and other shellfish are available from the chiller cabinets of many supermarkets. These tend to have a better flavour and texture than frozen seafood.

Finally, olive trees cover the centre and south of Italy and, as a result, olives and olive oil are plentiful, and the whole country has slopes covered in grapevines laden with delicious grapes. It is hardly surprising that Italy is one of the largest olive oil and wine producing countries in the world!

Traditionally, the main meal of the day in Italy is eaten at lunchtime and the average Italian family eats well. There are many courses in an Italian meal but not all are eaten on a regular basis and an everyday lunch is seldom an elaborate affair. It may start with antipasti, the food that comes before the meal. Its name comes from *ante*, meaning before, and *pasto*, meaning meal. Although often cold, there are also some hot antipasti and the selection of ingredients used is enormous. The intention is to stimulate the appetite and an antipasto may consist of just a few dishes such as a platter of prosciutto and a bowl of gherkins or olives, a wider selection of antipasti, occasionally a soup or salad, or something more substantial such as Tomato & Mozzarella Bruschetta. In Venice's wine bars antipasti known as *cicheti* are served.

A first course (il primo) always starts a meal and may consist of pasta, rice or gnocchi. These may seem rather substantial, but the servings are small and are followed by a simple meat or fish dish without numerous accompaniments.

It is often suggested that the explorer Marco Polo introduced pasta to Italy from China when he returned from his travels there but the Italians, particularly those in the south, were eating pasta long before then. Now it is eaten in almost every region and has become the most commonly eaten Italian dish, although it wasn't actually until the turn of the twentieth century that it became popular.

A light main course (il secondo) traditionally follows the first course. It usually consists of a small portion of meat, poultry, game or fish or, occasionally, a vegetable dish, accompanied by either a lightly cooked vegetable or a small salad. The main course is not as substantial as it is in many other cuisines and is cooked and served simply so that the full flavour of the food is appreciated. It is seldom covered in a sauce or served with numerous accompaniments.

At the end of an everyday Italian meal, a bowl of fresh seasonal fruit and a platter of local cheeses are usually served but desserts do feature in their cuisine. These are served for Sunday lunch, on special occasions, and at Christmas and Easter. More often their cakes and pastries are eaten at a café with mid-morning or afternoon cups of coffee. Italians are rightly famous for their refreshing ice creams and water ices, to be eaten at any time of day! In the evening, a lighter meal of antipasti, soup, omelette or a salad may be served. A cup of espresso, the national drink of Italy, settles the digestion and completes the Italian meal.

The Italians have a passion for their food. They say it's what life is all about! Let's hope that the recipes in this book will infect you with their enthusiasm. Buon appetito!

Caponata: This is a Sicilian speciality, which varies slightly from one part of the island to the other, but it always contains aubergine, onion, celery, tomato and capers. It is traditionally served at room temperature.

ingredients in the italian kitchen

Italy has an abundance of wonderful ingredients. The following are those that you will come across most frequently.

CHEESES

There are numerous Italian hard, semi-soft and fresh cheeses, but these are the most well known and readily available:

Bel Paese, literally translated, means beautiful country and is originally from the beautiful countryside of Lombardy in northern Italy. Made from cow's milk, it is soft and creamy and has a mild flavour. It can be eaten either on its own or used in a variety of cooked dishes.

Fontina is made in the Valle d'Aosta region and it takes its name from Monte Fontina near the Italian town of Aosta. Cheese that does not bear the description 'Fontina from the Valle d'Aosta' is not the genuine cheese. It is a semi-soft, full-fat cheese made from cow's milk. It has a delicate, nutty flavour and, because it melts evenly, it is a good cheese for cooking.

Gorgonzola is a blue-veined cheese, originally from the town of that name. It is made from cow's milk and has a buttery flavour. Gorgonzola Piccante has a sharp flavour and Gorgonzola Dolce is, as the name suggests, sweet. It melts well and is therefore often used in Italian sauces and in dishes such as Blue Cheese Risotto. Torta di San Gaudenzio is a cheese made from

layers of Gorgonzola and mascarpone. Dolcelatte is made from a combination of Gorgonzola and Italian cream cheese, and obviously has a milder, creamier flavour.

Mascarpone comes from southern Lombardy and is a soft cream cheese. It is used in desserts such as Tiramisù, Mascarpone Creams and Sweet Mascarpone Mousse, or can replace cream in sauces.

Mozzarella is a moist, semi-soft cheese moulded into spherical shapes. It has very good melting qualities when heated and is an essential ingredient for topping pizzas. It is also eaten fresh in salads, often with tomatoes and basil and drizzled with olive oil. Mozzarella was originally made with buffalo milk, and this variety has a superior flavour and is less rubbery in texture. Avoid mozzarella made outside of Italy as it is no substitute for the genuine product.

Parmesan is probably the most famous Italian cheese. Genuine Parmesan is made in and around the town of Parma and only then can it bear the name Parmigiano Reggiano, indicating that it is true Parmesan. It is used for grating on top of dishes such as pasta, risotto, polenta and soup, for shaving onto salads, as an ingredient in dishes such as in Lasagne al Forno, and can be eaten in chunks with bread or fruit. Parmesan belongs to a group of cheeses known as grana, meaning hard and grainy. Grana Padano belongs to the same group and is similar to Parmesan but is slightly inferior and less mature. Always buy fresh Parmesan for grating as pre-packed grated varieties do not compare in flavour.

Provolone, from the south of Italy, is recognized by its large pear-shape, covered in wax and hanging from a string. It is a curd cheese made from cow's milk and is sold fresh, or matured and hard, and can be eaten either way or used in cooking. Provola is a smaller version of provolone, as is caciocavallo, which looks like two saddlebags, and burrini, which are provola cheeses with unsalted butter in the centre.

Ricotta is a by-product of the whey, rather than the curd of milk. It is not really a cheese, but today whole or skimmed milk is added to it and it is sold as soft, white cheese. It has a bland flavour and is used to fill pasta and in desserts and tarts, especially in southern Italy and the islands of Sicily and Sardinia.

Taleggio is a semi-soft, cow's milk cheese that comes originally from the northern Italian Alps. It has a mild, sweet flavour and is best eaten when young as it reaches maturity after only six weeks.

PANCETTA

This is salted, spiced belly of pork, rolled into a large sausage shape and available either in one piece or very thinly sliced. When lean and thinly sliced it can be eaten like prosciutto but it is usually sliced or chopped and then fried, and used in savoury dishes such as soups, sauces and stuffings.

PROSCIUTTO

This is the Italian word for ham. Prosciutto cotto is cooked ham and prosciutto crudo is cured ham. Italy's most famous and popular cured ham is prosciutto di Parma and, like most Italian prosciutto, is air-dried for at least 8 months and sometimes for as long as 2 years. Genuine prosciutto di Parma comes from the area around the city of Parma in Emilia-Romagna and is produced from pigs fed on the whey from making Parmigiano Reggiano. It can be identified by the brand burned onto the skin. It is sliced thinly and should be pale red in colour, tender, with a sweet, smoky taste. Only salt is added to flavour it. It is traditionally served as antipasti, with melon, or in recipes such as Prosciutto & Figs. Prosciutto di San Danele is another equally good, if not better, Italian cured ham. It is pale pink in colour with a delicate flavour.

OLIVE OIL

Olive oil is made by crushing the flesh of olives before they turn black, and extracting the oil. Some of the best oil comes from Liguria – the flavour and texture of the oil become more intense the further south it is produced. The best olive oil should be heavy, a rich green in colour, and taste like green olives. Extra virgin olive oil is made

The soft, crumbly texture of Gorgonzola makes it ideal for use in cooking.

from the first pressing of the olives and is cold pressed, which means that the olives are crushed and the oil extracted without being heated or chemically treated. It has the best flavour and a maximum acidity of 1 per cent. Virgin olive oil has an acidity of no more than 1.5 per cent; olive oil or pure olive oil is made by using heat and/or pressing to extract the oil and it is then refined. Use your best oil for salads and drizzling over cooked dishes rather than in cooking, where its flavour will be lost and, once a bottle of oil has been opened, use it quite quickly to prevent it going off.

VINEGAR

Red and white vinegars are used in Italian cooking to prepare dressings, sauces and marinades, as is balsamic vinegar, which is also used sparingly in fish and meat dishes. Balsamic vinegar is made in Modena from sweet white Trebbiano di Spagna grapes by moving the vinegar from successively smaller barrels each year and blending very aged vinegars (up to 100 years old) with younger vinegars (no less than 12 years old). The barrels are manufactured from different aromatic and hard woods, such as old brandy barrels, and these too add flavour to the vinegar as it ages. This produces a rich, dark, syrupy vinegar and its production is protected by a consortium made up of the Modena families who produce it.

Balsamic vinegar between 40 and 50 years old is labelled *tradizionale*, while vinegar that is 10 or 12 years old is labelled *aceto balsamico di Modena*.

MARSALA

This is a fortified wine and can be dry, semi-dry or sweet. It is often used in Italian cooking and is the traditional ingredient in Zabaglione. It is also used in other desserts, such as Marsala Cherries, as well as in savoury dishes, particularly veal, pork and some risottos.

CAPERS

These are the little green buds of a low-growing wild shrub. They are an important ingredient in Italian cooking and are used whole or crushed, particularly in fish and veal dishes, sauces and stuffings. They are available preserved in brine or in vinegar, and those that come from Sicily are traditionally preserved in salt.

ANCHOVIES

Preserved anchovies are an essential ingredient in many Italian dishes, such as Bagna Cauda (see page 12). They are used to flavour sauces and are eaten as an antipasto. They can be found in supermarkets, canned or bottled in either oil or salt, and in delicatessens, preserved just in salt, and they can be whole or filleted. Those preserved in salt must be soaked for 30 minutes, rinsed and dried well, those canned or bottled in salt must be rinsed and those preserved in oil should be drained well before use.

PINE KERNELS

Umbrella pine trees grow in many parts of Italy but particularly in the Ligurian region in the north west. The kernels are extracted from the seeds found in the pine cones. They have a delicate flavour and are used in stuffings, salads, sprinkled over vegetables, in biscuits, cakes and in pesto sauce. Once opened, do not store for too long as they go off quickly.

CHESTNUTS

These grow in the mountainous areas of Italy and become widely available in the early months of winter. They are used in soups, stews and sweet dishes as well as being roasted and eaten whole. They are available fresh, vacuum-packed, canned and frozen.

CEPS

Known in Italy as *porcini*, these are wild boletus mushrooms. Although available fresh in spring and autumn, they are usually bought dried and have a highly concentrated flavour owing to the drying process. They must be soaked in water to reconstitute them before use and are ideal for flavouring risottos, sauces, soups, stuffings and meat dishes. They can also be added to dishes that contain fresh mushrooms to enhance their flavour.

TOMATOES

This vegetable dominates Italian cooking both as a flavouring and as a vegetable in its own right. Canned chopped tomatoes make an excellent substitute for fresh ones in cooked dishes (a 400 g/14 oz can is equivalent to about 1 kg/2 lb 4 oz fresh tomatoes) and in purée form they are excellent for flavouring dishes. No storecupboard should be without either.

GARLIC

Garlic is always associated with the cuisine of Italy but, in fact, not all its dishes are highly flavoured with it. Its reputation came about because most of the Italian emigrants to Britain and the United States came from southern Italy and more garlic is used in their cooking than anywhere else in Italy.

It is used with discretion in sauces and in meat, fish and vegetable dishes, and in certain classic dishes that rely on its flavour, such as Green Pesto Sauce.

OLIVES

These are the fruit of an evergreen tree and, depending on the region, the olives in Italy can be large, small, medium-sized, different shades of black or green, stoned or unstoned, stuffed or tossed in herbs. They are grown for eating on their own with aperitifs, in antipasti, in cooking and for turning into olive oil.

HERBS AND SPICES

Fresh herbs are used in Italian cooking whenever possible. Rosemary is the most popular herb in Tuscany and central Italy and is used to flavour roasted and grilled meat, particularly lamb and chicken. Sage is used mainly in the north in pork dishes and with calf's liver, and flat-leaved parsley is used extensively. Basil is probably the herb most associated with Italian cooking and is a vital ingredient in Green Pesto Sauce, giving it its vibrant green colour and distinctive flavour. Along with freshly ground black pepper, the most essential spice in the Italian kitchen is nutmeg. This is always used in spinach and ricotta dishes, both savoury and sweet. It should be freshly grated straight into the dish you are preparing.

Mushrooms are a popular ingredient in Italian cooking – the early morning autumn mists bring the mushroom-gatherers out in force, eager to find the best of the day's crop.

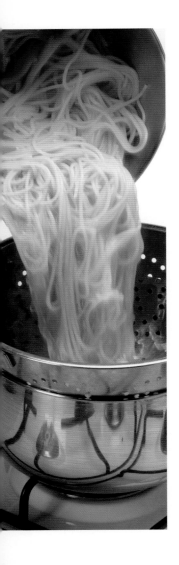

'OO' FLOUR

This flour is made from Italian soft durum wheat, which produces a strong flour rich in gluten. The wheat is very finely milled to produce 'OO' grade flour, which is soft and extra fine. It is mostly used to make fresh pasta as it is this high gluten content and the fineness of the flour that gives the pasta its true texture.

PASTA

The national dish of Italy, pasta is made from durum wheat flour, sometimes with the addition of egg and/or oil. It is available in numerous shapes and sizes, from the tiniest shells to large sheets of lasagne, and in different colours and flavours, for example spinach, tomato, beetroot, cuttlefish ink and herbs. In addition, the names of pasta shapes vary from region to region and from one manufacturer to another. At the last count there were over 650 varieties of pasta shapes. Pasta is available fresh or dried, or you can make it at home (see the Basic Pasta Dough recipe on page 25).

In this book, you will find a selection of pasta recipes served with a sauce. However, if you wish to use a shape of pasta other than the one specified in the recipe, although there are no hard and fast rules, there are some general guidelines, depending on the type of sauce. Short, tubular pasta, twists and shells, which have hollows and cavities for the sauce to cling to, are best served with chunky, thick sauces such as meat, fish and vegetable sauces, while long, thin pasta is best served with a simple smooth sauce such as Tomato Sauce or Green Pesto Sauce. The flatter the pasta the richer the sauce it should be eaten with, for example cream or cheese.

Always serve pasta dishes hot, and ideally in deep plates, to keep them warm and prevent any sauce served with them from splashing, and eat with a fork only – never a knife!

Cook's tips for cooking pasta

- Cook in the largest saucepan that you have in plenty of boiling water.

- Add the pasta to the water only when it is boiling and stir well at the beginning.

- You can add oil to the pasta water to prevent it from sticking, although this is not necessary.

- Cook at a rolling boil.

- Don't over-cook pasta. Dried pasta should still be firm to the bite or 'al dente'.

- Don't rinse the cooked pasta.

RICE

Most Italian rice is grown in the north, where rice paddies are part of the land-scape, and is classified by the size of the grain; originario, which is the smallest and is ideal for rice pudding, semifino, which includes varieties such as vialone and nano, fino and superfine, which is the longest and includes the arborio and carnaroli varieties. Only these specialized varieties should be used to make risotto, and each brings its own slightly different texture to the dish. It is the roundness and starchiness of the grain, which swells to at least three times its size while retaining a firm texture during cooking, that makes arborio and carnaroli rice ideal for making risottos. No other vari-ety of rice produces the same soft, creamy texture that is vital for a good risotto.

Cook's tips for cooking risotto

• Use a large shallow pan if possible so that the rice has room to expand.

• Use a wooden, rather than a metal spoon, as it is gentler and prevents damaging the texture of the rice.

• Keep the stock at simmering point so that it is about the same temperature as the rice.

• Stir the rice all the time while cooking, in a clockwise direction, not backwards and forwards, to prevent damaging the rice.

• Let a risotto stand for 2–3 minutes before serving to allow the flavours of the different ingredients to mingle.

SEMOLINA

This is ground durum wheat, which is available in different sized grains. Coarser grains are used to make semolina gnocchi and finer grains are used to make commercial dried pasta as it makes a tough dough that can be forced through dies to form shapes. It can also be used to sprinkle over freshly made pasta dough to prevent it from sticking together.

POLENTA

This is the name given both to an ingredient, which is ground corn, and to an Italian dish, which is a well-known speciality that is particularly popular in northern Italy. There are three varieties of cornmeal available, coarse, medium and fine, and the coarser the grain the yellower the colour. Coarse varieties are used to make polenta and finer varieties are better in cakes. Polenta is made by boiling it with water, stirring constantly for 40 minutes, to make a stiff

porridge. Instant polenta, which takes about 5 minutes to prepare, and ready-to-eat polenta are now available in supermarkets. Polenta has a bland flavour and is usually served with a strong-flavoured food or sauce or has ingredients added to it while it is cooking. It can also be fried or grilled after it has been turned out and become cold.

equipment for italian cooking

A basically equipped kitchen is all you need for Italian cooking but, apart from a set of sharp knives, wooden spoons, and a large pan for cooking pasta, there are some specialized pieces of equipment that make food preparation quicker and less demanding. You might consider purchasing some of the following pieces of equipment if you think that you might find them useful.

CITRUS ZESTER
This tool removes the zest of citrus fruit in long shreds without removing any bitter white pith. The zest is used for flavouring and decorating desserts and cakes.

GARLIC PRESS
Choose a good quality press for crushing the flesh and extracting the juice rather than chopping the garlic by hand.

ICE CREAM MAKER
These vary enormously in style and price but are worth investing in if you make a lot of ice cream or sorbets. There are manually-operated churns and several different models of electric ice cream makers that are better value, from those that work in the freezer to those that sit on the kitchen work surface and churn the mixture in a previously chilled container. Additionally, there are more expensive elec-

tric ice cream makers that are freestanding and have their own built-in freezing unit.

NUTMEG GRATER
Nutmeg should be used freshly ground and, as it is popular in Italian cooking, a nutmeg grater is to be found in every Italian kitchen.

MEZZALUNA
This semicircular knife is designed to rock backwards and forwards and is used for chopping ingredients such as herbs and nuts finely. It is often sold with a wooden board that has a dip in it. However, with the popularity of food processors its use has declined but you may find it useful for chopping small quantities and you have more control over the exact thickness of the food that you are chopping.

PARMESAN KNIFE
As mature Parmesan cheese is hard, Parmesan knives are designed not to cut, but to break off smaller pieces of cheese from a large piece and for scraping off slivers or slices.

PARMESAN GRATER
A special Parmesan grater is small and made of metal, so that you can grate the hard Parmesan cheese to exactly the right fineness required for sprinkling over a dish. A PARMESAN SHAVER, also made of metal, is used to shave the cheese.

PASTA MACHINE
These are convenient if you make a lot of pasta. A manual pasta machine rolls out and cuts the pasta dough into the size and shape that you require, such as sheets of lasagne or strips of tagliatelle. You can buy

extra attachments for some machines for making spaghetti and ravioli, and pasta-making attachments can be bought for some freestanding food mixers, which make different shapes such as spaghetti and macaroni. Electric pasta machines also mix the dough as well as rolling and cutting it but these machines are expensive and might be regarded as taking the enjoyment out of making pasta dough.

PASTA SCOOP
This sieve is ideal for scooping up long pasta such as spaghetti and comes in several designs. Some are metal spoons with a deep bowl, a slot in the base, and prongs around the edge and others are wooden spoons with prongs attached, sometimes called SPAGHETTI HOOKS.

PASTRY WHEEL
This is a small tool for cutting out pasta which, unlike a knife, does not drag the dough and gives a neat edge. It is particularly good for cutting out stuffed pasta such as ravioli.

PESTLE AND MORTAR
Often made of marble, these are used for crushing garlic and grinding peppercorns and spices. Choose a deep mortar with a rough inner surface to help with grinding.

PIZZA PAN
Made of metal with a perforated base, this is used for cooking a pizza in the oven so that the base remains crisp. A PIZZA STONE is preheated in the oven before the pizza is placed on it to cook. It absorbs moisture and helps produce the results of a professional pizza oven.

PIZZA WHEEL
This tool has a sharp circular blade which is used for slicing pizza without tearing it.

POLENTA EQUIPMENT
When polenta is cooked, it splutters and spits a lot and must be stirred constantly. A wooden spoon with a long handle is therefore essential to prevent it from burning you. If you make a lot of polenta, a PAIOLO, a copper pot with deep sides, is useful. A preserving pan or a deep, heavy-based saucepan are good alternatives.

RAVIOLI EQUIPMENT
A RAVIOLI CUTTER is a small tool with a wooden handle that has a square or round metal cutter attached. It is used to cut out individual pieces of ravioli. A RAVIOLI ROLLING PIN is a wooden pin with indentations in it that shape the squares of ravioli as you roll it over the dough and a RAVIOLI TRAY or GRID is a metal tray made up of about 36 squares over which the rolled out dough is placed, after which the squares are filled, a second piece of dough is placed on top and, finally, a rolling pin is rolled over the top to make individual squares.

ROLLING PIN
A long, heavy wooden rolling pin is essential for rolling out pasta thinly. Italian rolling pins are at least 70 cm/28 in long.

SALAD DRAINER
This may come in the form of a wire basket with a handle, which is shaken, or a plastic container with a basket that fits inside, which is spun by pulling a string or turning a knob on the lid. Both are excellent for drying washed salad leaves thoroughly.

makes 1 quantity

basic pizza dough

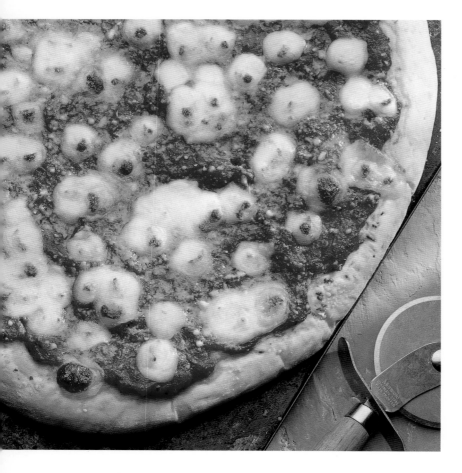

INGREDIENTS
15 g/½ oz dried yeast
1 tsp sugar
250 ml/9 fl oz hand-hot water
350 g/12 oz strong white flour
1 tsp salt
1 tsp olive oil

1 Put the yeast and sugar in a measuring jug and mix with 50 ml/2 fl oz of the water. Leave the mixture in a warm place for 15 minutes or until frothy.

2 In a large bowl, mix the flour with the salt and make a well in the centre. Add the oil, the yeast mixture and the remaining water. Using a wooden spoon, mix together to form a smooth dough.

3 Turn the dough out onto a floured work surface and knead it for 4–5 minutes until it is smooth.

4 Return the dough to the bowl, cover with a clean, damp tea towel and leave to rise in a warm place for 30 minutes or until the dough has doubled in size.

5 Knead the dough for 2 minutes then stretch it with your hands to form a round no more than 5 mm/¼ in thick. Place it on an oiled baking tray, pushing out the edges until even.

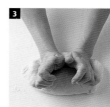

makes 1 quantity

basic pasta dough

INGREDIENTS
280 g/10 oz strong white flour, preferably '00' grade, plus extra for dusting
1 tsp salt
1 tbsp olive oil
2 eggs, lightly beaten

1 Lightly dust a work surface with flour. Sift the flour and salt into a mound onto the work surface.

2 Make a well in the centre of the flour, add the oil and beaten eggs and, using your fingertips, work to form a stiff dough. If necessary, add 2–3 tablespoons water to make the dough pliable.

3 Knead the dough vigorously for 8–10 minutes until the dough is smooth, firm and soft. Wrap the dough in a plastic bag or clingfilm and leave it to rest in the refrigerator for 30 minutes.

4 Divide the dough into 2 equal pieces. Cover a work surface with a clean cloth or tea towel and dust it liberally with flour. Place one portion of the dough on the floured cloth and roll it out as thinly and evenly as possible, stretching the dough gently until the pattern of the weave shows through. Cover the rolled dough with a cloth while rolling out the second piece. Alternatively, use a pasta machine to roll the dough.

5 Using a ruler and a sharp-bladed knife, or a pasta or pastry wheel, cut the pasta into the required shapes, such as lasagne or tagliatelle, or use a pasta machine to form the dough into shapes.

6 To dry the pasta, place a tea towel over the back of a chair and hang the strips over it for 30–45 minutes to become partly dry.

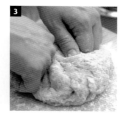

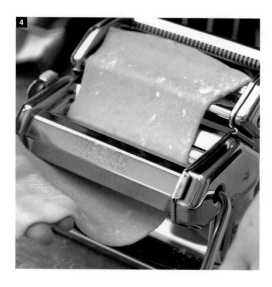

makes 300 ml/½ **pint**

basic tomato sauce

INGREDIENTS
2 tbsp olive oil
1 small onion, chopped
1 garlic clove, chopped
400 g/14 oz canned chopped tomatoes
2 tbsp chopped fresh parsley
1 tsp dried oregano
2 bay leaves
2 tbsp tomato purée
1 tsp sugar
salt and pepper

1 Heat the oil in a saucepan over a medium heat, add the onion and fry for 2–3 minutes or until translucent. Add the garlic and fry for 1 minute.

2 Stir in the tomatoes, parsley, oregano, bay leaves, tomato purée, sugar and salt and pepper to taste.

3 Bring the sauce to the boil, then simmer, uncovered, for 15–20 minutes or until the sauce has reduced by half. Taste the sauce and adjust the seasoning if necessary. Discard the bay leaves just before serving. This sauce keeps well in a screw-top jar in the refrigerator for up to 1 week.

makes 600 ml/1 pint

béchamel sauce

INGREDIENTS
300 ml/½ pint milk
2 bay leaves
3 cloves
1 small onion
55 g/2 oz butter, plus extra for greasing
40 g/1½ oz plain flour
300 ml/½ pint single cream
large pinch of freshly grated nutmeg
salt and pepper

1 Pour the milk into a small suacepan and add the bay leaves. Press the cloves into the onion, add to the saucepan and bring the milk to the boil. Remove the saucepan from the heat and set aside to cool.

2 Strain the milk into a jug and rinse the saucepan. Melt the butter in the saucepan, stir in the flour and cook for 1 minute, stirring. Remove from the heat and gradually pour in the milk, stirring constantly. Cook the sauce for 3 minutes, stirring, then pour in the cream and bring it to the boil. Remove from the heat and season with nutmeg, salt and pepper to taste.

makes 125 ml/4 fl oz

green pesto sauce

INGREDIENTS
40 fresh basil leaves
3 garlic cloves, crushed
25 g/1 oz pine kernels
50 g/1¾ oz Parmesan cheese, finely grated
2–3 tbsp extra virgin olive oil
salt and pepper

1 Rinse the basil leaves and pat them dry with kitchen paper. Put the basil leaves, garlic, pine kernels and Parmesan into a food processor and blend for 30 seconds or until smooth. Alternatively, pound all of the ingredients in a mortar with a pestle.

2 If you are using a food processor, keep the motor running and slowly add the olive oil. Alternatively, add the oil drop by drop while stirring briskly. Season with salt and pepper to taste.

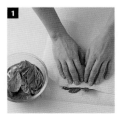

makes 2 litres/3½ pints

chicken stock

INGREDIENTS
1 kg/2 lb 4 oz chicken, skinned
2 celery sticks
1 large onion
2 carrots
1 garlic clove
fresh parsley sprigs
2 litres/3½ pints water
salt and pepper

1 Put all the ingredients into a large saucepan and bring to the boil over a medium heat.

2 Using a slotted spoon skim any scum from the surface. Reduce the heat to a gentle simmer, partially cover and cook for 2 hours, then leave to cool.

3 Line a sieve with clean muslin and place over a large jug or bowl. Pour the stock through the sieve. The cooked chicken can be used in another recipe. Discard the other solids. Cover the stock and chill in the refrigerator.

4 Store in the refrigerator for 3–4 days until required, or freeze in small batches. Before using, skim off any fat that has formed.

makes 2 litres/3½ pints

vegetable stock

INGREDIENTS
250 g/9 oz shallots
1 large carrot, diced
1 celery stick, chopped
½ fennel bulb
1 garlic clove
1 bay leaf
fresh parsley sprigs
fresh tarragon sprigs
2 litres/3½ pints water
pepper

1 Put all the ingredients into a large saucepan and bring to the boil over a medium heat.

2 Using a slotted spoon skim any scum from the surface. Reduce the heat to a gentle simmer, partially cover and cook for 45 minutes, then let cool.

3 Line a sieve with clean muslin and place over a large jug or bowl. Pour the stock through the sieve. Discard the herbs and the vegetables.

4 Cover and store in small quantities in the refrigerator for up to 3 days. The stock can also be frozen in small quantities.

part one

ANTIPASTI
appetizers, soups & salads

There is a variety of antipasti to suit all tastes in this section. Choose just a few, a whole selection, or even serve the more substantial dishes as a light meal, if preferred.

Soups are ideal for serving as a light beginning to a meal or as a meal in themselves, and the same applies to the salad recipes that follow. You are spoilt for choice!

serves 4 | prep 10 mins | cook 45 mins

crostini alla fiorentina

Serve as part of an antipasto, or spread on small pieces of fried crusty bread (crostini) as an appetizer with drinks.

INGREDIENTS
3 tbsp olive oil
1 onion, chopped
1 celery stick, chopped
1 carrot, chopped
1–2 garlic cloves, crushed
125 g/4½ oz chicken livers
125 g/4½ oz calf's, lamb's or pig's liver
150 ml/5 fl oz red wine
1 tbsp tomato purée
2 tbsp chopped fresh parsley, plus extra
  to garnish
3–4 canned anchovy fillets, finely chopped
2 tbsp stock or water
2–3 tbsp butter
1 tbsp capers
salt and pepper
small pieces of fried crusty bread, to serve

Heat the oil in a saucepan, add the onion, celery, carrot and garlic, and cook gently for 4–5 minutes or until the onion has become soft but not coloured.

Meanwhile, rinse and dry the chicken livers. Dry the calf's liver and slice into strips. Add the liver to the saucepan and fry gently for a few minutes until the strips are well sealed on all sides.

Add half of the wine and cook until it has mostly evaporated. Then add the rest of the wine, tomato purée, half of the parsley, the anchovy fillets, stock or water, a little salt and plenty of pepper.

Cover the saucepan and leave to simmer, stirring occasionally, for 15–20 minutes or until the liver is tender and most of the liquid has been absorbed.

Leave the mixture to cool a little, then either mince coarsely or put into a food processor and process to a chunky purée.

Return to the saucepan and add the butter, capers and remaining parsley. Heat through gently until the butter melts. Adjust the seasoning and turn out into a bowl. Serve warm or cold spread on the slices of crusty bread and sprinkled with chopped parsley.

serves 4 | prep 10 mins | cook 50 mins

leek & tomato timbales

Angel-hair pasta, known as cappellini, is mixed with fried leeks, sun-dried tomatoes, fresh oregano and beaten eggs, and baked in ramekins.

INGREDIENTS
90 g/3¼ oz angel-hair pasta (cappellini)
2 tbsp butter
1 tbsp olive oil
1 large leek, finely sliced
60 g/2¼ oz sun-dried tomatoes in oil,
　drained and chopped
1 tbsp chopped fresh oregano
　or 1 tsp dried oregano
2 eggs, beaten
100 ml/3½ fl oz single cream
1 tbsp freshly grated Parmesan
salt and pepper
sprigs of oregano, to garnish
lettuce leaves, to serve

tomato sauce
1 small onion, finely chopped
1 small garlic clove, crushed
350 g/12 oz tomatoes, peeled (see Cook's
　Tip on page 111) and chopped
1 tsp mixed dried Italian herbs
4 tbsp dry white wine

Cook the pasta in plenty of boiling salted water for about 3 minutes until just tender but still 'al dente'. Drain and rinse with cold water to cool quickly.

Meanwhile, heat the butter and oil in a frying pan. Gently fry the leek until softened, about 5–6 minutes. Add the sun-dried tomatoes and oregano, and cook for a further 2 minutes. Remove from the heat.

Add the leek mixture to the pasta. Stir in the beaten eggs, cream and Parmesan. Season with salt and pepper. Divide between four greased ramekin dishes or dariole moulds.

Place the dishes in a roasting tin with enough warm water to come halfway up their sides. Bake in a preheated oven, 180°C/350°F/Gas Mark 4, for about 30 minutes, until the mixture has set.

Meanwhile, make the tomato sauce. Fry the onion and garlic in the remaining butter and oil until softened. Add the tomatoes, herbs and wine. Cover and cook gently for about 20 minutes until pulpy. Blend in a food processor until smooth, or press through a sieve.

Run a knife or small spatula around the edge of the ramekins, then turn out the timbales onto four warm serving plates. Pour over a little sauce and garnish with oregano. Serve with the lettuce leaves.

serves 4 | prep 10 mins | cook 25 mins

tuna-stuffed tomatoes

Deliciously sweet roasted tomatoes are filled with home-made lemon mayonnaise and tuna.

INGREDIENTS
4 plum tomatoes
2 tbsp sun-dried tomato purée
2 egg yolks
2 tsp lemon juice
finely grated rind of 1 lemon
4 tbsp olive oil
115g/4 oz canned tuna, drained
2 tbsp capers, rinsed
salt and pepper

to garnish
2 sun-dried tomatoes, cut into strips
fresh basil leaves

Halve the tomatoes and scoop out the seeds. Divide the sun-dried tomato purée among the tomato halves and spread around the inside of the skin.

Place on a baking tray and roast in a preheated oven at 200°C/400°F/Gas Mark 6 for 12–15 minutes. Leave to cool slightly.

Meanwhile, make the mayonnaise. In a food processor, blend the egg yolks and lemon juice with the lemon rind until smooth. Once mixed and with the motor still running slowly, add the olive oil. Stop the processor as soon as the mayonnaise has thickened. Alternatively, use a hand whisk, beating the mixture continuously until it thickens.

Add the tuna and capers to the mayonnaise and season.

Spoon the tuna mayonnaise mixture into the tomato shells and garnish with sun-dried tomato strips and basil leaves. Return to the oven for a few minutes or serve chilled.

COOKS TIP
For a picnic, do not roast the tomatoes, just scoop out the seeds, drain, cut-side down, on absorbent kitchen paper for 1 hour, and fill with the mayonnaise mixture. They are firmer and easier to handle this way. If you prefer, shop-bought mayonnaise may be used instead – just stir in the lemon rind.

serves 4 | prep 10 mins | cook 8 mins

avocado margherita

Heat the olive oil in a frying pan. Add the onion and garlic and fry gently for 2 minutes or until soft.

Peel the tomatoes, using the method described in the Cook's Tip on page 111.

Arrange the avocado halves on a plate with the narrow ends pointed towards the centre. Spoon the onion mixture into the hollow of each half.

Cut and slice the tomatoes in half. Divide the tomatoes, basil and thin slices of mozzarella between the avocado halves. Season with salt and pepper to taste.

Place the avocado halves under a preheated medium grill for 5–6 minutes or until the avocados are heated through and the cheese has melted. Transfer the avocados to serving plates, garnish with basil leaves and serve with mixed salad leaves.

The colours of the tomatoes, basil and mozzarella cheese in this patriotic recipe represent the colours of the Italian flag.

VARIATION
If you are using a combination microwave oven with grill, arrange the avocados on the low rack of the grill, or on the glass turntable. Cook on combination grill 1 and LOW power for 8 minutes until the tops are browned and bubbling.

INGREDIENTS
1 tbsp olive oil
1 small red onion, sliced
1 garlic clove, crushed
2 small tomatoes
2 avocados, halved and stoned
4 fresh basil leaves, torn into shreds
60 g/2 oz mozzarella cheese, thinly sliced
salt and pepper
fresh basil leaves, to garnish
mixed salad leaves, to serve

serves 4 | prep 10 mins | cook 10 mins

tomato & mozzarella bruschetta

These simple toasts are filled with colour and flavour. They are delicious as a speedy appetizer or as a light meal or snack.

INGREDIENTS
4 muffins
4 garlic cloves, crushed
2 tbsp butter
1 tbsp chopped basil
4 large, ripe tomatoes, peeled
  (see Cook's Tip on page 111)
1 tbsp tomato purée
8 stoned black olives, halved
50 g/1¾ oz mozzarella cheese, sliced
salt and pepper
fresh basil leaves, to garnish

dressing
1 tbsp olive oil
2 tsp lemon juice
1 tsp clear honey

Cut the muffins in half to give eight thick pieces. Toast the muffin halves under a hot grill for 2–3 minutes until golden.

Mix the garlic, butter and basil together and spread onto each muffin half.

Chop the tomato flesh and mix with the tomato purée and olives. Divide the mixture between the muffins.

Mix the dressing ingredients and drizzle over each muffin.

Place a slice of mozzarella cheese on top of each muffin and season.

Return the muffins to the grill for 1–2 minutes until the cheese melts.

Garnish with fresh basil leaves and serve at once.

VARIATION
Use balsamic vinegar instead of the lemon juice for a deliciously authentic Italian flavour.

serves 4 | prep 5 mins | cook 40 mins

fried risotto balls

The Italian name for this dish translates as 'telephone wires', which refers to the strings of melted mozzarella cheese contained within the risotto balls.

INGREDIENTS
2 tbsp olive oil
1 medium onion, finely chopped
1 garlic clove, chopped
½ red pepper, diced
150 g/5½ oz risotto rice, washed
1 tsp dried oregano
375 ml/13 fl oz hot Vegetable or Chicken Stock (see page 29)
100 ml/3½ fl oz dry white wine
75 g/2¾ oz mozzarella cheese
oil, for frying
fresh basil sprig, to garnish

Heat the oil in a frying pan and cook the onion and garlic for 3–4 minutes or until just softened.

Add the red pepper, rice and oregano to the frying pan. Cook for 2–3 minutes, stirring to coat the rice in the oil.

Mix the stock together with the wine and add to the frying pan a ladleful at a time, waiting for the liquid to be absorbed by the rice before you add the next ladleful of liquid.

Once all of the liquid has been absorbed and the rice is tender (it should take about 15 minutes in total), remove the frying pan from the heat and leave until the mixture is cool enough to handle.

Cut the cheese into 12 pieces. Taking about 1 tablespoon of risotto, shape the mixture around the cheese pieces to make 12 balls.

Heat the oil until a cube of bread browns in 30 seconds. Cook the risotto balls, in batches of four, for 2 minutes or until golden.

Remove the risotto balls with a slotted spoon and drain thoroughly on absorbent kitchen paper. Garnish with a sprig of basil and serve the risotto balls hot.

VARIATION
For an even cheesier flavour, stir in a tablespoon of grated Parmesan cheese before taking the risotto off the heat.

serves 4 | prep 20 mins | cook 30 mins

pancetta & pecorino cakes

These cakes also make an excellent light meal when served with a topping of pesto or anchovy sauce.

INGREDIENTS
2 tbsp butter, plus extra for greasing
100 g/3½ oz pancetta, rind removed
225 g/8 oz self-raising flour
75 g/2¾ oz grated pecorino cheese
150 ml/5 fl oz milk, plus extra for glazing
1 tbsp tomato ketchup
1 tsp Worcestershire sauce
400 g/14 oz dried farfalle
1 tbsp olive oil
salt
3 tbsp Green Pesto Sauce (see page 28)
  or anchovy sauce (optional)
green salad, to serve

Grease a baking tray with butter. Grill the pancetta until it is cooked. Allow the pancetta to cool, then chop finely.

Sift together the flour and a pinch of salt into a mixing bowl. Add the butter and rub in with your fingertips. When the butter and flour have been thoroughly incorporated, add the pancetta and one-third of the grated cheese.

Mix together the milk, tomato ketchup and Worcestershire sauce and add to the dry ingredients, mixing to make a soft dough. Roll out the dough on a lightly floured board to make an 18-cm/7-inch round. Brush with a little milk to glaze and cut into eight wedges.

Arrange the dough wedges on the prepared baking tray and sprinkle over the remaining cheese. Bake in a preheated oven at 200°C/400°F/Gas Mark 6 for 20 minutes.

Meanwhile, bring a saucepan of lightly salted water to the boil. Add the farfalle and the oil and cook for 8–10 minutes until just tender, but still 'al dente'. Drain and transfer to a large serving dish. Top with the pancetta and pecorino cakes. Serve with the sauce of your choice and a green salad.

serves 4 | prep 10 mins + 20 mins chilling | cook 0 mins

prosciutto with figs

This classic Italian appetizer couldn't be easier or more delicious. Paper-thin prosciutto di Parma has a uniquely aromatic flavour. Succulent fresh figs make a natural partnership.

INGREDIENTS
175 g/6 oz prosciutto di Parma,
   thinly sliced
4 fresh figs
1 lime
2 fresh basil sprigs
pepper

Using a sharp knife, trim the visible fat from the slices of ham and discard. Arrange the ham on 4 large serving plates, loosely folding it so that it falls into decorative shapes. Season to taste with pepper.

Using a sharp knife, cut each fig lengthways into four wedges. Arrange a fig on each serving plate. Cut the lime into six wedges, place a wedge on each plate and reserve the others. Remove the leaves from the basil sprigs and divide between the plates. Cover with clingfilm and chill in the refrigerator until ready to serve.

Just before serving, remove from the refrigerator and squeeze the juice from the remaining lime wedges over the prosciutto.

VARIATION
This dish is also delicious made with four slices of Charentais melon or 12–16 cooked and cooled asparagus spears, instead of the figs.

makes 16–30 | prep 10 mins | cook 20 mins

courgette fritters

These tasty little fritters are a good one-dish antipasto and are great served as finger food at a drinks party.

Sift the flour into a large bowl and make a well in the centre. Add the eggs to the well and, using a wooden spoon, gradually draw in the flour.

Slowly add the milk to the mixture, stirring constantly to form a thick batter.

Meanwhile, wash the courgettes. Grate them over a sheet of kitchen paper placed in a bowl to absorb some of the juices.

Add the courgettes, thyme and salt and pepper to taste to the batter and mix together thoroughly.

Heat the oil in a large, heavy-based frying pan. Taking a tablespoon of the batter for a medium-sized fritter or half a tablespoon of batter for a smaller fritter, spoon the mixture into the hot oil and cook, in batches, for 3–4 minutes on each side.

Remove the fritters with a slotted spoon and drain thoroughly on absorbent kitchen paper. Keep each batch of fritters warm in the oven while making the rest. Transfer to serving plates and serve hot.

INGREDIENTS
100 g/3½ oz self-raising flour
2 eggs, beaten
50 ml/2 fl oz milk
300 g/10½ oz courgettes
2 tbsp fresh thyme
1 tbsp oil
salt and pepper

VARIATION
Try adding ½ teaspoon of dried, crushed chillies to the batter with the thyme for spicier fritters.

serves 4 | prep 5 mins + 15 mins marinating | cook 0 mins

marinated raw beef

You need extremely thin slices of meat for this recipe. If you place the beef in the freezer for about 30 minutes, you will find it easier to slice.

INGREDIENTS
200 g/7 oz fillet of beef, in 1 piece
2 tbsp lemon juice
4 tbsp extra virgin olive oil
55 g/2 oz Parmesan cheese, thinly shaved
4 tbsp chopped fresh flat-leaved parsley
salt and pepper
lemon slices, to garnish
ciabatta or focaccia, to serve

VARIATION
To make Carpaccio di Tonno, substitute fresh, uncooked tuna for the fillet of beef. Do not use thawed frozen fish, and eat on the day of purchase.

Using a very sharp knife, cut the beef fillet into wafer-thin slices and arrange on four individual serving plates.

Pour the lemon juice into a small bowl and season to taste with salt and pepper. Beat in the olive oil, then pour the dressing over the meat. Cover the plates with clingfilm and set aside for 10–15 minutes to marinate.

Remove and discard the clingfilm. Arrange the Parmesan shavings in the centre of each serving and sprinkle with parsley. Garnish with lemon slices and serve with fresh bread.

serves 4 | prep 5 mins | cook 0 mins

prosciutto with rocket

Rocket has become a fashionable salad vegetable in many homes and restaurants, but it has never been out of favour in Italy, where it grows wild.

INGREDIENTS
115 g/4 oz rocket
1 tbsp lemon juice
3 tbsp extra virgin olive oil
225 g/8 oz prosciutto, thinly sliced
salt and pepper

Separate the rocket leaves, wash in cold water and pat dry on kitchen paper. Place the leaves in a bowl.

Pour the lemon juice into a small bowl and season to taste with salt and pepper. Beat in the olive oil, then pour the dressing over the rocket leaves and toss lightly so they are evenly coated.

Carefully drape the prosciutto in folds on 4 individual serving plates, then add the rocket. Serve at room temperature.

VARIATION
For a more substantial salad, add 1 thinly sliced fennel bulb and 2 thinly sliced oranges for the rocket. Substitute orange juice or balsamic vinegar for the lemon juice.

serves 4 | prep 10 mins | cook 0 mins

italian platter

This popular hors d'oeuvre usually consists of vegetables soaked in olive oil and rich, creamy cheeses. Try this great low-fat version as a guilt-free appetizer.

INGREDIENTS
125 g/4½ oz reduced-fat mozzarella
   cheese, drained
60 g/2¼ oz lean prosciutto di Parma
400 g/14 oz canned artichoke hearts, drained
4 ripe figs
1 small mango
few plain bread sticks, to serve

dressing
1 small orange
1 tbsp passata
1 tsp wholegrain mustard
4 tbsp low-fat natural yogurt
fresh basil leaves
salt and pepper

Cut the cheese into 12 sticks, 6 cm/2½ inches long. Remove the fat from the ham and slice the meat into 12 strips. Carefully wrap a strip of ham around each stick of cheese and arrange on a serving platter.

Halve the artichoke hearts, cut the figs into quarters and arrange them on the platter

Peel the mango, then slice it down each side of the large, flat central stone. Slice the flesh into strips and arrange them to form a fan shape on the serving platter.

To make the dressing, pare the rind from half of the orange using a vegetable peeler.

Cut the rind into small strips and place them in a bowl. Extract the juice from the orange and add it to the bowl containing the rind.

Add the passata, mustard, yogurt and seasoning to the bowl and mix together. Shred the basil leaves into small pieces and mix them into the dressing.

Spoon the dressing into a small dish and serve with the Italian Platter, accompanied with bread sticks.

serves 6 | prep 15 mins | cook 0 mins

antipasto volente

In Italy, antipasti are served as appetizers before the pasta course. The name of this dish translates as 'take your pick'.

INGREDIENTS
200 g/7 oz canned tuna in oil, drained and
    flaked into chunks
115 g/4 oz canned sardines in
    oil, drained
100 g/3½ oz canned anchovy fillets
    in oil, drained
175 g/6 oz cooked peeled
    prawns, deveined
115 g/4 oz prosciutto, cut into strips
175 g/6 oz mozzarella cheese, sliced
390 g/13½ oz canned artichoke hearts,
    drained and halved lengthways
3 fresh figs, sliced
225 g/8 oz canned asparagus
    spears, drained
115 g/4 oz smoked salmon, thinly sliced
10 black olives, stoned
extra virgin olive oil, for drizzling
salt and pepper
lemon wedges, to garnish

Arrange the tuna, sardines, anchovies, prawns, prosciutto, mozzarella, artichoke hearts and figs on a large serving platter.

Wrap two to three asparagus spears in each slice of smoked salmon and add to the platter. Season the antipasto to taste with salt and pepper.

Sprinkle the olives over the platter and drizzle with the olive oil. Garnish with lemon wedges, then serve immediately or cover with clingfilm and chill in the refrigerator until required, but bring to room temperature before serving.

VARIATION
If you like, use the same amount of fresh asparagus spears instead of canned. Steam or cook in boiling water for 5–7 minutes, or until tender.

serves 4 | prep 10 mins | cook 25 mins

caponata

This is a Sicilian speciality, which varies slightly from one part of the island to the other, but it always contains aubergine, onion, celery, tomato and capers. It is traditionally served at room temperature.

INGREDIENTS
4 tbsp olive oil
1 onion, sliced
2 celery sticks, sliced
1 aubergine, diced
5 plum tomatoes, chopped
1 garlic clove, finely chopped
3 tbsp red wine vinegar
1 tbsp sugar
12 black olives, stoned
2 tbsp capers
salt
3 tbsp chopped fresh flat-leaved parsley,
    to garnish

Heat 2 tablespoons of the olive oil in a large, heavy-based saucepan. Add the onion and celery and cook over a low heat, stirring frequently, for 5 minutes, or until softened. Add the remaining oil with the aubergine and cook, stirring constantly, for 10 minutes.

Stir in the tomatoes, garlic, vinegar and sugar. Cover the surface of the caponata with a circle of greaseproof paper and simmer for 10 minutes.

Stir in the olives and capers and season to taste with salt. Transfer the mixture to a serving dish and leave to cool to room temperature. Serve, sprinkled with parsley.

VARIATION
If you are not cooking for vegetarians, add four anchovies with the capers. Desalt them by soaking them in a little milk for 5 minutes before using.

serves 6 | prep 15 mins | cook 30 mins

polenta with prosciutto

These are ideal appetizers when you are entertaining, as they can be prepared in advance and then popped under the grill when you are ready to serve.

INGREDIENTS
600 ml/1 pint water
200 g/7 oz quick-cook polenta
50 g/1¾ oz freshly grated Parmesan cheese
2 tbsp butter, softened
salt and pepper

topping
2 tbsp extra virgin olive oil, plus extra for greasing and to serve
6 slices prosciutto
85 g/3 oz fontina cheese, cut into 6 slices
12 fresh sage leaves

Line a 5 x 25-cm/6 x 10-inch Swiss roll tin with baking parchment and set aside.

Pour the measured water into a large saucepan and bring to the boil. Reduce the heat so that it is just simmering and add a large pinch of salt. Add the polenta in a steady stream, stirring constantly. Simmer, stirring, for 5 minutes, until thickened.

Remove the saucepan from the heat, stir in the Parmesan and butter and season to taste with pepper. Spoon the polenta evenly into the saucepan and smooth the surface with a spatula. Set aside to cool.

Oil a baking tray and a 7.5-cm/3-inch plain, round pastry cutter. Turn out the

polenta, stamp out circles and place on the baking tray. Brush with olive oil and season with salt and pepper.

Cook under a preheated grill for 3–4 minutes. Turn the circles over, brush with more oil and grill for an additional 3–4 minutes, until golden. Remove from the grill and, if you are not serving immediately, set the circles aside to cool.

Drape a slice of ham on each polenta circle and top with a slice of fontina. Brush the sage leaves with some of the remaining olive oil and place two on each polenta circle.

Cook the polenta circles under a preheated grill for 3–4 minutes, until the cheese has melted and the sage is crisp. Serve immediately with extra olive oil for dipping.

serves 4 | prep 20 mins | cook 1 hr

roman artichokes

The Roman contribution to this dish of stuffed artichokes is to flavour it with mint. Italian or Roman mint has a particularly sweet flavour, but you could use garden mint or one of the more exciting varieties, such as lemon or apple mint.

INGREDIENTS
5 tbsp lemon juice
4 globe artichokes
1 garlic clove
4 sprigs fresh flat-leaved parsley
2 sprigs fresh mint
1 lemon, cut into quarters
4 tbsp olive oil
2 tbsp dry, uncoloured breadcrumbs
2 garlic cloves, finely chopped
25 g/1 oz fresh flat-leaved parsley,
    coarsely chopped
25 g/1 oz fresh mint, coarsely chopped
1 tbsp unsalted butter, diced
salt and pepper

Select a bowl large enough to accommodate the prepared artichokes and fill with cold water and 4 tablespoons of the lemon juice. Working on one artichoke at a time, snap off the stems, then peel away the tough outer leaves. Snip or break off the tough tops of the remaining leaves. When the central cone of the artichoke appears, cut off the top 2 cm/¾ inches with a sharp knife. Drop the prepared artichokes into the acidulated water to prevent them discolouring.

Place the artichokes in a heavy-based saucepan that is large enough to hold them firmly upright in a single layer. Add the whole garlic clove, parsley sprigs, mint sprigs, lemon quarters and olive oil, and season to taste with salt and pepper. Pour in enough water to come two-thirds of the way up the sides of the saucepan. Bring to the boil over a low heat, cover tightly and simmer for about 15 minutes, until the artichokes are nearly tender.

Meanwhile, combine the breadcrumbs, chopped garlic, parsley and mint in a bowl, and season to taste with salt and pepper.

Remove the artichokes from the saucepan and set aside to cool slightly. When they are cold enough to handle, gently separate the leaves, remove the central bearded chokes or cones with a teaspoon and discard. Season the artichokes to taste with salt and pepper. Return them to the saucepan, again standing them upright in a single layer. Spoon the breadcrumb mixture into the centres, cover tightly and cook over a low heat for 20–30 minutes, until tender.

Using a slotted spoon, transfer the artichokes to four individual serving plates and set aside. Strain the cooking liquid into a clean saucepan and bring to the boil over a high heat. Cook until reduced by about one-quarter or until the juices are concentrated, then reduce the heat and stir in the remaining lemon juice. Add the butter, a piece at a time, swirling the sauce in the saucepan until the butter has melted. Do not let the sauce boil. When all the butter has been incorporated, remove the saucepan from the heat. Serve the artichokes still warm and hand round the sauce separately.

serves 6 | prep 45 mins | cook 2 hrs 15 mins

minestrone

There are as many variations of this classic Italian soup as there are Italian cooks. You can use almost any vegetable in season to make minestrone. You can also add a little lean bacon to give the soup more body. *

INGREDIENTS
2 fresh basil sprigs
2 fresh marjoram sprigs
2 fresh thyme sprigs
2 tbsp olive oil
2 onions, chopped
2 garlic cloves, chopped
4 tomatoes, peeled (see Cook's Tip on page 111) and chopped
225 ml/8 fl oz red wine
2 litres/3½ pints Vegetable Stock (see page 29)
175 g/6 oz cannellini beans, soaked overnight in cold water, then drained
2 carrots, chopped
2 potatoes, chopped
1 small turnip, chopped
1 celery stick, chopped
¼ small cabbage, shredded
55 g/2 oz dried soup pasta shapes
salt and pepper
25 g/1 oz freshly grated Parmesan cheese, plus extra to serve

Chop enough fresh basil, marjoram and thyme to fill 2 tablespoons and reserve until required. Heat the olive oil in a heavy-based saucepan. Add the onions and cook, stirring occasionally, for 5 minutes, or until softened. Stir in the garlic and cook for an additional 3 minutes, then stir in the chopped tomatoes and the reserved herbs.

Add the wine, simmer for 1–2 minutes, then add the stock and drained beans. Bring to the boil, then reduce the heat, partially cover and simmer for 1½ hours.

Add the carrots, potatoes and turnip, then cover and simmer for 15 minutes. Add the celery, cabbage and pasta, then cover and simmer for an additional 10 minutes. Season to taste with salt and pepper and stir in the Parmesan cheese. Ladle into warmed bowls and serve with extra Parmesan cheese.

COOK'S TIP
*If you are a meat-eater you can add 2 slices of pancetta, or Italian bacon, rinded and chopped, to the soup with the garlic. It is available from Italian delicatessens and adds an extra depth of flavour to the soup.

serves 4 | prep 10 mins | cook 25 mins

creamy tomato soup

Soup made from fresh tomatoes is nothing like canned or packaged soups and is destined to become a family favourite.

INGREDIENTS
55 g/2 oz butter
1 onion, finely chopped
700 g/1 lb 9 oz tomatoes,
  finely chopped
600 ml/1 pint hot Chicken
  or Vegetable Stock (see page 29)
pinch of sugar
90 ml/3 fl oz single cream
25 g/1 oz shredded fresh basil leaves
1 tbsp chopped fresh parsley
salt and pepper

Melt half the butter in a large, heavy-based saucepan. Add the onion and cook over a low heat, stirring occasionally, for 5 minutes, or until softened. Add the tomatoes, season to taste with salt and pepper and cook for 5 minutes.

Pour in the hot stock, return to the boil, reduce the heat and cook for 10 minutes.

Push the soup through a sieve with the back of a wooden spoon to remove the tomato skins and seeds.

Return to the saucepan and stir in the sugar, cream, remaining butter, basil and parsley. Heat through briefly, but do not boil. Ladle the soup into warmed bowls and serve immediately.

VARIATION
Replace the chopped fresh parsley with the same amount of chopped fresh chives and serve with freshly grated Parmesan cheese sprinkled on the top.

serves 4 | prep 1 hr + 6 hrs chilling | cook 5 hrs

beef soup with eggs

Good-quality, homemade beef consommé is essential for this unusual soup. It is best to make it 24 hours in advance so that you can remove every trace of fat from the surface of the consommé.

INGREDIENTS
500 g/1 lb 2 oz beef marrow bones, sawn
   into 7.5-cm/3-inch pieces
350 g/12 oz stewing beef, in 1 piece
1.4 litres/2½ pints water
4 cloves
2 onions, halved
2 celery sticks, coarsely chopped
8 peppercorns
1 bouquet garni

to serve
55 g/2 oz unsalted butter
4 slices fresh white bread
115 g/4 oz freshly grated Parmesan cheese
4 eggs
salt and pepper

First, make the consommé. Place the bones in a large, heavy-based saucepan with the stewing beef on top. Add the water and bring to the boil over a low heat, skimming off all the scum that rises to the surface. Pierce a clove into each onion half and add to the saucepan with the celery, peppercorns and bouquet garni. Partially cover and simmer very gently for 3 hours. Remove the meat and simmer for a further hour.

Strain the consommé into a bowl and set aside to cool. When completely cold, chill in the refrigerator for at least 6 hours, preferably overnight. Carefully remove and discard the layer of fat that has formed on the surface. Return the consommé to a clean saucepan and heat until almost boiling.

When you are ready to serve, melt the butter in a heavy-based frying pan. Add the bread, one slice at a time if necessary, and cook over a medium heat until crisp and golden on both sides. Remove from the frying pan and place one each in the base of four warmed soup bowls.

Sprinkle half the Parmesan over the fried bread. Carefully break an egg* over each slice of fried bread, keeping the yolks whole. Season to taste with salt and pepper and sprinkle with the remaining Parmesan. Carefully ladle the hot consommé into the soup bowls and serve immediately.

COOK'S TIP
*If you prefer, you could lightly poach the eggs before placing them on the fried bread slices.

serves 4 | prep 15 mins | cook 2 hrs 50 mins

white bean soup

Beans feature widely in Tuscan cuisine. This smooth, comforting soup, in which beans are simmered for 2 hours, is very simple to make. Garlic and parsley, stirred in just before serving, complement the flavour, and a drizzle of olive oil adds the final touch.

Drain the soaked beans and place them in a large, heavy-based saucepan. Add the stock and bring to the boil. Partially cover the saucepan, reduce the heat and simmer for 2 hours, until tender.

Transfer about half the beans and a little of the stock to a food processor or blender and process to a smooth purée. Return the purée to the pan and stir well to mix. Bring the soup back to the boil.

Add the pasta to the soup, bring back to the boil and cook for 10 minutes, until tender.

Meanwhile, heat 4 tablespoons of the olive oil in a small saucepan. Add the garlic and cook over a low heat, stirring frequently, for 4–5 minutes, until golden. Stir the garlic into the soup and add the parsley. Season to taste with salt and pepper and ladle into warmed soup bowls. Drizzle with the remaining olive oil and serve immediately.

VARIATION
Substitute borlotti beans for the cannellini beans and cook for about 1½ hours.

INGREDIENTS
175 g/6 oz dried cannellini beans, covered and soaked overnight in cold water
1.7 litres/3 pints Chicken or Vegetable Stock (see page 29)
115 g/4 oz soup pasta
6 tbsp olive oil
2 garlic cloves, finely chopped
4 tbsp chopped fresh flat-leaved parsley
salt and pepper

serves 4 | prep 5 mins | cook 3hrs 15 mins

veal & ham soup

Veal and ham is a classic combination, complemented here with the addition of cream sherry to create a richly-flavoured Italian soup.

INGREDIENTS
4 tbsp butter
1 onion, diced
1 carrot, diced
1 celery stick, diced
450 g/1 lb veal, very thinly sliced
450 g/1 lb ham, thinly sliced
50 g/2 oz plain flour
1 litre/1¾ pints beef stock
1 bay leaf
8 black peppercorns
pinch of salt
3 tbsp redcurrant jelly
150 ml/5 fl oz pint cream sherry
100g/3½ oz dried vermicelli
garlic croûtons,* to serve

Melt the butter in a large saucepan. Add the onions, carrot, celery, veal and ham and cook over a low heat for 6 minutes.

Sprinkle over the flour and cook, stirring constantly, for a further 2 minutes. Gradually stir in the stock, then add the bay leaf, peppercorns and salt. Bring to the boil and simmer for 1 hour.

Remove the pan from the heat and add the redcurrant jelly and cream sherry, stirring to combine. Set aside for about 4 hours.

Remove the bay leaf from the saucepan and discard. Reheat the soup over a very low heat until warmed through.

Meanwhile, cook the vermicelli in a saucepan of lightly salted boiling water for 10–12 minutes. Stir the vermicelli into the soup and transfer to soup bowls. Serve with garlic croûtons.

COOK'S TIP
To make garlic croûtons, remove the crusts from 3 slices of day-old white bread. Cut the bread into 5-mm/¼-inch cubes. Heat 3 tablespoons oil over low heat and stir-fry 1–2 chopped garlic cloves for 1–2 minutes. Remove the garlic and add the bread. Cook, stirring frequently, until golden. Remove with a slotted spoon and drain.

serves 4 | prep 20 mins | cook 35 mins

seafood soup

Full of delicious Mediterranean flavours, this soup is both less heavy and much easier to make than its French Provençal cousin bouillabaisse.

INGREDIENTS
4 tbsp olive oil
1 garlic clove, sliced
2 tbsp chopped fresh flat-leaved parsley
1 dried red chilli, whole
200 g/7 oz canned plum tomatoes, chopped
1 cod or haddock head
125 ml/4 fl oz dry white wine
850 ml/1½ pints boiling water
450 g/1 lb monkfish fillet
280 g/10 oz live mussels
450 g/1 lb raw prawns
salt and pepper
4 slices sfilatino or French bread,
    each 2 cm/¾ inch thick, to serve

Heat half the olive oil in a large, heavy-based saucepan. Add the garlic, half the parsley and the chilli and cook over a low heat, stirring occasionally, for 3 minutes, until the garlic starts to colour. Add the tomatoes, fish head and wine and continue to cook until almost all the liquid has gone. Add the boiling water, season with salt and simmer for 20 minutes.

Meanwhile, remove the grey membrane from the monkfish and cut the flesh into bite-sized pieces. Scrub the mussels under cold running water and tug off the beards. Discard any mussels with broken or damaged shells and those that do not shut immediately when sharply tapped. Peel the prawns, cut a slit along the back of each and remove and discard the dark vein.

Add the monkfish and mussels to the saucepan and simmer for 4–5 minutes. Add the prawns and simmer for 2–3 minutes, until they have changed colour.

Remove and discard the fish head and the chilli. Remove any mussels that have not opened. Add the remaining olive oil and parsley to the soup, taste and adjust the seasoning if necessary.

Toast the bread and put a slice in the base of 4 warmed soup bowls. Ladle the soup over the bread and serve immediately.

serves 4 | prep 2 mins | cook 10 mins

tuscan bean soup

A thick and creamy soup that is based on a traditional Tuscan recipe. If you use dried beans, the preparation and cooking times will be longer.

INGREDIENTS
225 g/8 oz dried butter beans, soaked overnight, or 2 x 400 g/14 oz cans butter beans
1 tbsp olive oil
2 garlic cloves, crushed
1 vegetable or chicken stock cube, crumbled
150 ml/5 fl oz milk
2 tbsp chopped fresh oregano
salt and pepper

If you are using dried beans that have been soaked overnight, drain them thoroughly. Bring a large saucepan of water to the boil, add the beans and boil for 10 minutes. Cover the saucepan and simmer for a further 30 minutes or until tender. Drain the beans, reserving the cooking liquid. If you are using canned beans, drain them thoroughly and reserve the liquid.

Heat the oil in a large frying pan and fry the garlic for 2–3 minutes or until just beginning to brown.

Add the beans and 375 ml/13 fl oz of the reserved liquid to the frying pan, stirring constantly. You may need to add a little water if there is insufficient liquid. Stir in the crumbled stock cube. Bring the mixture to the boil, stirring, and then remove the frying pan from the heat.

Place the bean mixture in a food processor and blend to form a smooth paste. Alternatively, mash the bean mixture to a smooth consistency. Season to taste with salt and pepper and stir in the milk.

Pour the soup back into the frying pan and gently heat to just below boiling point. Stir in the chopped oregano just before serving.

serves 8 | prep 15 mins | cook 1 hr 45 mins

genoese vegetable soup

*This classic vegetable soup is served
with an equally classic pesto sauce that
originated in the Ligurian port of Genoa.
It makes a wonderful dish for an informal
dinner with family and friends.*

INGREDIENTS
2 onions, sliced
2 carrots, diced
2 celery sticks, sliced
2 potatoes, diced
115 g/4 oz French beans, cut into
    2.5-cm/1-inch lengths
115 g/4 oz peas, thawed if frozen
200 g/7 oz fresh spinach leaves, coarse stalks
    removed, shredded
2 courgettes, diced
225 g/8 oz Italian plum tomatoes, peeled
    (see Cook's Tip on page 111), deseeded
    and diced
3 garlic cloves, thinly sliced
4 tbsp extra virgin olive oil
2 litres/3½ pints Vegetable or Chicken Stock
    (see page 29)
140 g/5 oz dried stellete or other soup pasta
1 quantity Green Pesto Sauce (see page 28)
salt and pepper
freshly grated Parmesan cheese, to serve

Put the onions, carrots, celery, potatoes, beans, peas, spinach, courgettes, tomatoes and garlic in a large, heavy-based saucepan, pour
in the olive oil and stock and bring to the boil over a medium-low
heat. Reduce the heat and simmer gently for about 1½ hours.

Season the soup to taste with salt and pepper and add the pasta.
Cook for an additional 8–10 minutes, until the pasta is tender, but
still firm to the bite. The soup should be very thick.

Stir in half the Green Pesto Sauce, remove the saucepan from
the heat and set aside to rest for 4 minutes. Taste and adjust
the seasoning, adding more salt, pepper and Green Pesto Sauce
if necessary.

Ladle into warmed bowls and serve immediately. Hand round the
freshly grated Parmesan cheese separately.

VARIATION
*Instead of soup pasta, add 140 g/5 oz
cooked long-grain rice just before the
end of the cooking time and continue
cooking the soup just long enough to
heat the rice through before setting the
soup aside to rest.*

serves 4 | prep 20 mins | cook 5 mins

capri salad

This tomato, olive and mozzarella salad, dressed with balsamic vinegar and olive oil, makes a delicious antipasto.

INGREDIENTS
2 beef tomatoes
125 g/4½ oz fresh mozzarella cheese, drained
12 black olives
1 tbsp balsamic vinegar
1 tbsp olive oil
salt and pepper
basil leaves, to garnish

Using a sharp knife, cut the tomatoes into thin slices.

Using a sharp knife, cut the mozzarella into slices.

Stone the olives and slice them into rings.

Layer the tomato, mozzarella cheese and olives in a stack, finishing with a layer of cheese on top.

Place each stack under a preheated hot grill for 2–3 minutes or just long enough to melt the mozzarella.

Drizzle over the vinegar and olive oil, and season to taste with a little salt and pepper.

Transfer to serving plates and garnish with basil leaves. Serve immediately.

serves 4 | prep 15 mins | cook 1 hr 45 mins

beans with tuna

This is a truly mouthwatering dish that has been horribly corrupted by cheap trattorie that are no more Italian than a sushi bar. Forget any ghastly memories of canned beans and tuna and try the real thing. For hungry people you might allow one tuna steak each, but the beans are very filling.

INGREDIENTS
800 g/1 lb 12 oz cannellini beans,
   covered and soaked overnight in cold water
6 tbsp extra virgin olive oil
2 x 200 g/7 oz tuna steaks
2 garlic cloves, lightly crushed
sprig fresh sage
2 tbsp water
salt and pepper
4 chopped fresh sage leaves, to garnish

Drain the soaked beans and place them in a saucepan. Add enough water to cover and bring to the boil. Reduce the heat and simmer for 1–1½ hours, until tender. Drain the beans thoroughly.

Heat 1 tablespoon of the olive oil in a heavy-based frying pan. Add the tuna steaks and cook over a medium heat for 3–4 minutes on each side. Remove from the frying pan and set aside to cool.

Heat 3 tablespoons of the remaining olive oil in a heavy-based frying pan. Add the garlic and sage sprig and cook briefly over a low heat until the sage starts to sizzle. Remove the garlic and discard.

Add the beans and cook for 1 minute, then add the measured water and season to taste with salt and pepper. Cook until the water has been absorbed. Remove and discard the sage sprig, transfer the beans to a bowl and set aside to cool.

Meanwhile, flake the tuna, removing any bones. When the beans are lukewarm or at room temperature, according to taste, gently stir in the tuna. Drizzle with the remaining olive oil, sprinkle with the chopped sage and serve.

serves 4 | prep 15 mins | cook 0 mins

artichoke & rocket salad

This simple Tuscan salad is made from the small, tender artichokes of the early summer. The tart flavour of the lemons is perfectly complemented by the saltiness of the pecorino cheese.

INGREDIENTS
8 baby globe artichokes
juice of 2 lemons
100 g/3½ oz rocket
125 ml/4 fl oz extra virgin olive oil
115 g/4 oz pecorino cheese
salt and pepper

Break off the stems of the artichokes and cut off about 2.5 cm/ 1 inch of the tops, depending on how young and small they are. Remove and discard any coarse outer leaves, leaving only the pale, tender inner leaves. Using a teaspoon scoop out the chokes. Rub each artichoke with lemon juice as soon as it is prepared to prevent it from discolouring.

Thinly slice the artichokes and place in a salad bowl. Add the rocket, lemon juice and olive oil, season to taste with salt and pepper and toss well.

Using a swivel-blade vegetable peeler, thinly shave the pecorino over the salad, then serve immediately.

VARIATION
This salad can also be made from the artichoke's close relation, the cardoon. Cut off and discard the tough, outer stalks.

serves 4 | prep 15 mins + 8 hrs chilling | cook 0 mins

layered tomato salad

This is a very popular salad throughout Italy and an excellent way of using up yesterday's bread. For the fullest flavour, use sun-ripened tomatoes.

INGREDIENTS
1 red onion, thinly sliced into rings
4 slices day-old bread
115 g/4 oz black olives, stoned and
  thinly sliced
450 g/1 lb tomatoes, thinly sliced
115 g/4 oz fresh mozzarella cheese, drained
  and thinly sliced
1 tbsp shredded fresh basil
125 ml/4 fl oz extra virgin olive oil
3 tbsp balsamic vinegar
4 tbsp lemon juice
salt and pepper

VARIATION
To enhance the flavour of the tomatoes chop 25 g/1 oz sundried tomatoes over the salad before serving.

Place the onion slices in a bowl and add cold water to cover. Set aside to soak for 10 minutes. Meanwhile, dip the slices of bread in a shallow dish of cold water, then squeeze out the excess. Place the bread in a serving dish. Slice the olives thinly.

Drain the onion slices and layer them on the bread with the tomatoes and mozzarella, sprinkling each layer with the basil and salt and pepper.

Pour over the olive oil, vinegar and lemon juice, and sprinkle with the olives. Cover and chill for up to 8 hours before serving.

serves 4 | prep 15 mins | cook 10 mins

goat's cheese, pear & walnut salad

In this popular combination of ingredients the delicate flavour of the goat's cheese combines beautifully with the sweet pears and slightly bitter walnuts.

INGREDIENTS
250 g/9 oz dried penne
1 head radicchio, torn into pieces
1 Webbs lettuce, torn into pieces
7 tbsp chopped walnuts
2 ripe pears, cored and diced
115 g/4 oz rocket, trimmed
2 tbsp lemon juice
5 tbsp olive oil
1 garlic clove, chopped
3 tbsp white wine vinegar
4 tomatoes, quartered
1 small onion, sliced
1 large carrot, grated
250 g/9 oz goat's cheese, diced

Bring a large saucepan of lightly salted water to the boil over a medium heat. Add the pasta and cook until done. Drain the pasta thoroughly and refresh in cold water, then drain again and set aside to cool.

Put the radicchio and Webbs lettuce into a large salad bowl and mix together well. Top with the cooled pasta, chopped walnuts, pears and rocket.

Mix the lemon juice, oil, garlic and vinegar together in a measuring jug. Pour the mixture over the salad ingredients and toss to coat the salad leaves well.

Add the tomato quarters, onion slices, grated carrot and diced goat's cheese and toss together with two forks, until well mixed. Chill the salad in the refrigerator for about 1 hour before serving.

COOK'S TIP
Most goat's cheese comes from France and there are many varieties, such as Crottin de Chavignol, Chabi, which is very pungent, and Sainte-Maure, which comes in creamery and farmhouse varieties.

serves 4 | prep 5 mins + 30 mins chilling | cook 0 mins

insalata tricolore

With the white mozzarella, red tomatoes and green basil representing the colours of the Italian flag, this salad is served all over Italy and beyond.

INGREDIENTS
280 g/10 oz fresh mozzarella cheese, drained
  and thinly sliced
8 plum tomatoes, sliced
20 fresh basil leaves
125 ml/4 fl oz extra virgin olive oil
salt and pepper

Arrange the cheese and tomato slices on 4 individual serving plates and season to taste with salt. Set aside in a cool place for 30 minutes.

Sprinkle the basil leaves over the salad and drizzle with the olive oil. Season with pepper and serve immediately.

VARIATION
There are dozens of variations of this popular and refreshing salad. Add 24 stoned black olives and 5 drained and chopped anchovies before adding the basil. Alternatively, peel, halve and stone 2 avocados. Cut the flesh crossways into thin slices and arrange them over the salad before sprinkling with the basil. Thinly slice a small white and a small red onion and push out into rings. Arrange them on top of the salad before sprinkling with the basil.

part two

PRIMI PIATTI
pasta & rice

Pasta and rice are served as a first course in the
Italian menu but there is no reason why you can't
serve them as a meal on their own, accompanied
by a salad. Many Italians eat these dishes every
day, so it is no wonder there are so many different
recipes to ring the changes.

serves 4 | prep 15 mins | cook 8–10 mins

pasta with pesto

Home-made pesto is much more delicious than even good-quality, shop-bought brands and it makes a wonderful no-cook sauce for all types of freshly cooked pasta.

INGREDIENTS
450 g/1 lb dried spaghetti
1 quantity Green Pesto Sauce
  (see page 28)
fresh basil sprigs, to garnish (optional)

Bring a large heavy-based saucepan of lightly salted water to the boil. Add the pasta, return to the boil, and cook for 8–10 minutes, until the pasta is tender but still 'al dente'. Drain, reserving 1–2 tablespoons of the cooking water.

If you like, thin the Green Pesto Sauce slightly with the cooking water, then add to the pasta and toss well. Transfer to warmed serving bowls and serve immediately, garnished with basil, if using.

VARIATION
For a green pesto with a completely different flavour, replace the basil in the Green Pesto Sauce with a large bunch of rocket, about 100 g/3½ oz.

serves 4 | prep 10 mins | cook 8–10 mins

tagliatelle with walnuts

This unusual combination would make an intriguing appetizer for a dinner party, but is also great for a light lunch, if served with a crisp green salad and crusty bread.

INGREDIENTS
25 g/1 oz fresh white breadcrumbs
350 g/12 oz walnut pieces
2 garlic cloves, finely chopped
4 tbsp milk
4 tbsp olive oil
85 g/3 oz fromage frais or cream cheese
150 ml/5 fl oz single cream
350 g/12 oz dried tagliatelle
salt and pepper

Place the breadcrumbs, walnuts, garlic, milk, olive oil and cream cheese in a large mortar and grind to a smooth paste. Alternatively, place the ingredients in a food processor and process until smooth. Stir in the cream to give a thick sauce consistency and season to taste with salt and pepper. Set aside.

Bring a large heavy-based saucepan of lightly salted water to the boil. Add the pasta, return to the boil and cook for 8–10 minutes, or until tender but still 'al dente'.

Drain the pasta and transfer to a warmed serving dish. Add the walnut sauce and toss thoroughly to coat. Serve immediately.

serves 4 | prep 5 mins | cook 15 mins

spaghetti olio & aglio

*Cooked pasta gets cold quickly, so make
sure that the serving dish is warmed
thoroughly, and as soon as the pasta is
drained, transfer to the dish.*

INGREDIENTS
450 g/1 lb dried spaghetti
125 ml/4 fl oz extra virgin olive oil
3 garlic cloves, finely chopped
3 tbsp chopped fresh
   flat-leaved parsley
salt and pepper

Bring a large, heavy-based saucepan of
lightly salted water to the boil. Add the
spaghetti, return to the boil and cook for
8–10 minutes, until the pasta is tender but
still 'al dente'.

Meanwhile, heat the olive oil in a heavy-
based frying pan. Add the garlic and a pinch
of salt and cook over a low heat, stirring
constantly, for 3–4 minutes, or until golden.
Do not allow the garlic to brown or it
will taste bitter. Remove the frying pan
from the heat.

Drain the pasta and transfer to a warmed
serving dish. Pour in the garlic-flavoured
olive oil, then add the chopped parsley
and season to taste with salt and pepper.
Toss well and serve immediately.

serves 6 | prep 15 mins | cook 45 mins

spaghetti with meatballs

Every Italian mamma has her own version of this dish, which, naturally, is the best.

INGREDIENTS
1 potato, diced
400 g/14 oz minced steak
1 onion, finely chopped
1 egg
4 tbsp chopped fresh flat-leaved parsley
plain flour, for dusting
5 tbsp virgin olive oil
400 ml/14 fl oz passata
2 tbsp tomato purée
400 g/14 oz dried spaghetti
salt and pepper

to garnish
6 fresh basil leaves, shredded
freshly grated Parmesan cheese

Place the potato in a small saucepan, add cold water to cover and a pinch of salt, and bring to the boil. Cook for 10–15 minutes, until tender, then drain. Either mash thoroughly with a potato masher or fork or pass through a potato ricer.

Combine the potato, steak, onion, egg and parsley in a bowl and season to taste with salt and pepper. Spread out the flour on a plate. With dampened hands, shape the meat mixture into walnut-sized balls and roll in the flour. Shake off any excess.

Heat the oil in a heavy-based frying pan, add the meatballs and cook over a medium heat, stirring and turning frequently, for 8–10 minutes, until golden all over.

Add the passata and tomato purée and cook for an additional 10 minutes, until the sauce is reduced and slightly thickened.

Meanwhile, bring a large saucepan of lightly salted water to the boil. Add the pasta, bring back to the boil, and cook for 8–10 minutes, until the pasta is tender, but still 'al dente'.

Drain well and add to the meatball sauce, tossing well to coat. Transfer to a warmed serving dish, garnish with the basil leaves and Parmesan and serve immediately.

serves 4 | prep 20 mins | cook 40 mins

macaroni with roasted vegetables

Roasting Mediterranean vegetables brings out their sweetness and full flavour to make a naturally rich sauce for pasta.

INGREDIENTS
2 red onions, cut into wedges
2 courgettes, cut into chunks
1 red pepper, deseeded and
    cut into chunks
1 yellow pepper, deseeded and
    cut into chunks
1 aubergine, cut into chunks
450 g/1 lb plum tomatoes,
    cut into quarters and deseeded
3 garlic cloves, chopped
4 tbsp olive oil
350 g/12 oz dried short-cut macaroni
350 ml/12 fl oz passata
12 black olives, stoned and halved
salt and pepper

to garnish
fresh basil sprigs
fresh flat-leaved parsley sprigs

Preheat the oven to 240°C/475°F/Gas Mark 9. Spread out the onions, courgettes, peppers, aubergine and tomatoes in a single layer in a large roasting tin. Sprinkle with the garlic, drizzle with the olive oil and season to taste with salt and pepper. Stir well until all the vegetables are coated. Roast in the preheated oven for 15 minutes, then remove from the oven and stir well. Return to the oven for 15 minutes.

Bring a large heavy-based saucepan of lightly salted water to the boil. Add the pasta, return to the boil and cook for 8–10 minutes, or until the pasta is tender but still 'al dente'.

Meanwhile, transfer the roasted vegetables to a large heavy-based saucepan and add the passata and olives. Heat through gently, stirring occasionally. Drain the pasta and transfer to a warmed serving dish. Add the roasted vegetable sauce and toss well. Garnish with the fresh basil and parsley and serve immediately.

VARIATION
Other vegetables would work very well in this dish, such as bite-sized pieces of butternut squash, and cherry tomato halves.

serves 4 | prep 10 mins | cook 12 mins

bavettine with smoked salmon & rocket

Do not overcook the salmon or rocket; they should just be warmed through and the rocket lightly wilted. If rocket is unavailable, replace it with baby spinach leaves.

INGREDIENTS
350 g/12 oz dried bavettine
2 tbsp olive oil
1 garlic clove, finely chopped
115 g/4 oz smoked salmon, cut into
   thin strips
55 g/2 oz rocket
salt and pepper
½ lemon, to garnish

Bring a large, heavy-based saucepan of lightly salted water to the boil. Add the pasta, return to the boil and cook for 8–10 minutes, or until tender but still 'al dente'.

Just before the end of the cooking time, heat the olive oil in a heavy-based frying pan. Add the garlic and cook over a low heat, stirring constantly, for 1 minute. Do not allow the garlic to brown or it will taste bitter. Add the salmon and rocket. Season to taste with salt and pepper and cook, stirring constantly, for 1 minute. Remove the frying pan from the heat.

Drain the pasta and transfer to a warmed serving dish. Add the smoked salmon and rocket mixture, toss lightly and serve, garnished with a lemon half.

serves 4 | prep 15 mins | cook 1hr 15 mins

lasagne al forno

*Layers of pasta, meat sauce and lasagne,
all covered with a rich cheese sauce, makes
a tasty and substantial family supper.*

INGREDIENTS
2 tbsp olive oil
55 g/2 oz pancetta or rindless
   lean bacon, chopped
1 onion, chopped
1 garlic clove, finely chopped
225 g/8 oz fresh minced beef
2 celery stalks, chopped
2 carrots, chopped
pinch of sugar
½ tsp dried oregano
400 g/14 oz canned chopped tomatoes
225 g/8 oz dried no-precook lasagne
225 g/8 oz freshly grated Parmesan cheese,
   plus extra for sprinkling
salt and pepper

cheese sauce
2 tsp Dijon mustard
70 g/2½ oz Cheddar cheese, grated
70 g/2½ oz Gruyère cheese, grated
300 ml/10 fl oz hot Béchamel Sauce
   (see page 27)

VARIATION
*Substitute the Gruyère cheese with
another good melting cheese, such as
Emmenthal, if you prefer.*

Preheat the oven to 190°C/375°F/Gas Mark 5. Heat the olive oil in a large, heavy-based saucepan. Add the pancetta and cook over a medium heat, stirring occasionally, for 3 minutes, or until the fat starts to run. Add the onion and garlic and cook, stirring occasionally, for 5 minutes, or until softened.

Add the beef and cook, breaking it up with a wooden spoon, until browned all over. Stir in the celery and carrot and cook for 5 minutes. Season to taste with salt and pepper. Add the sugar, oregano and tomatoes and their can juices. Bring to the boil, reduce the heat and simmer for 30 minutes.

Meanwhile, to make the cheese sauce, stir the mustard and both cheeses into the hot Béchamel Sauce.

In a large, rectangular ovenproof dish, make alternate layers of meat sauce, lasagne and Parmesan cheese. Pour the cheese sauce over the layers, covering them completely, and sprinkle with Parmesan cheese. Bake in the preheated oven for 30 minutes, or until golden brown and bubbling. Serve immediately.

serves 4 | prep 15 mins | cook 1 hr 25 mins

pork & pasta bake

When cooking with olive oil, there is no need to use extra virgin olive oil as the flavour will be lost during cooking. Olive oil is best stored in a cool place, out of direct sunlight, but not in the refrigerator.

INGREDIENTS
2 tbsp olive oil
1 onion, chopped
1 garlic clove,
   finely chopped
2 carrots, diced
55 g/2 oz pancetta, chopped
115 g/4 oz mushrooms, chopped
450 g/1 lb minced pork
125 ml/4 fl oz dry white wine
4 tbsp passata
200 g/7 oz canned chopped tomatoes
2 tsp chopped fresh sage
   or ½ tsp dried sage
225 g/8 oz dried elicoidali
140 g/5 oz mozzarella cheese, diced
4 tbsp freshly grated Parmesan cheese
300 ml/10 fl oz hot Béchamel Sauce
   (see page 27)
salt and pepper

Preheat the oven to 200°C/400°F/Gas Mark 6. Heat the olive oil in a large, heavy-based frying pan. Add the onion, garlic and carrots and cook over a low heat, stirring occasionally, for 5 minutes, or until the onion has softened. Add the pancetta and cook for 5 minutes. Add the chopped mushrooms and cook, stirring occasionally, for an additional 2 minutes. Add the pork and cook, breaking it up with a wooden spoon, until the meat is browned all over. Stir in the wine, passata, chopped tomatoes and their can juices and sage. Season to taste with salt and pepper and bring to the boil, then cover and simmer over a low heat for 25–30 minutes.

Meanwhile, bring a large, heavy-based saucepan of lightly salted water to the boil. Add the pasta, return to the boil and cook for 8–10 minutes, or until tender but still 'al dente'.

Spoon the pork mixture into a large oven-proof dish. Stir the mozzarella and half the Parmesan cheese into the Béchamel Sauce. Drain the pasta and stir the sauce into it, then spoon it over the pork mixture. Sprinkle with the remaining Parmesan cheese and bake in the oven for 25–30 minutes, or until golden brown. Serve the bake immediately.

serves 4 | prep 15 mins | cook 1hr 40 mins

pasticcio

This recipe shares its origins with a traditional Greek bake made with lamb. It is delicious served hot or cold.

INGREDIENTS
1 tbsp olive oil
1 onion, chopped
2 garlic cloves, finely chopped
450 g/1 lb minced lamb
2 tbsp tomato purée
2 tbsp plain flour
350 ml/12 fl oz Chicken Stock
  (see page 29)
1 tsp ground cinnamon
115 g/4 oz dried short-cut macaroni
2 beef tomatoes, sliced
350 ml/12 fl oz Greek-style yogurt
2 eggs, lightly beaten
salt and pepper

Preheat the oven to 190°C/375°F/Gas Mark 5. Heat the olive oil in a large heavy-based frying pan. Add the onion and garlic and cook over a low heat, stirring occasionally, for 5 minutes, or until softened. Add the lamb and cook, breaking it up with a wooden spoon, until browned all over. Add the tomato purée and sprinkle in the flour. Cook, stirring, for 1 minute, then stir in the Chicken Stock. Season to taste with salt and pepper and stir in the cinnamon. Bring to the boil, reduce the heat, cover and cook for 25 minutes.

Meanwhile, bring a large heavy-based saucepan of lightly salted water to the boil. Add the pasta, return to the boil, and cook for 8–10 minutes, or until tender but still 'al dente'.

Spoon the lamb mixture into a large oven-proof dish and arrange the tomato slices on top. Drain the pasta and transfer to a bowl. Add the yogurt and eggs and mix well. Spoon the pasta mixture on top of the lamb and bake in the preheated oven for 1 hour. Serve immediately.

VARIATION
Pasticcio is also delicious made with minced turkey or chicken. Replace the Greek-style yogurt with natural yogurt, if you like.

serves 4 | prep 15 mins | cook 1hr 45 mins

chicken & wild mushroom cannelloni

Cannelloni tubes filled with a delicious mix of exotic mushrooms, chicken and prosciutto make a wonderful dinner party main course. Serve with a crisp green salad, if you like.

INGREDIENTS
butter, for greasing
2 tbsp olive oil
2 garlic cloves, crushed
1 large onion, finely chopped
225 g/8 oz exotic mushrooms, sliced
350 g/12 oz minced chicken
115 g/4 oz prosciutto, diced
150 ml/5 fl oz Marsala
200 g/7 oz canned chopped tomatoes
1 tbsp shredded fresh basil leaves
2 tbsp tomato purée
10–12 cannelloni tubes
600 ml/1 pint Béchamel Sauce
  (see page 27)
100 g/3½ oz freshly grated
  Parmesan cheese
salt and pepper

Preheat the oven to 190°C/375°F/Gas Mark 5. Lightly grease a large ovenproof dish. Heat the olive oil in a heavy-based frying pan. Add the garlic, onion and mushrooms, and cook over a low heat, stirring frequently, for 8–10 minutes. Add the chicken and prosciutto and cook, stirring frequently, for 12 minutes, or until browned all over. Stir in the Marsala, tomatoes and their can juices, basil and tomato purée, and cook for 4 minutes. Season to taste with salt and pepper, then cover and simmer for 30 minutes. Uncover, stir and simmer for 15 minutes.

Meanwhile, bring a large heavy-based saucepan of lightly salted water to the boil. Add the pasta, return to the boil, and cook for 8–10 minutes, or until tender but still 'al dente'. Transfer the cannelloni tubes to a plate with a slotted spoon and pat dry with kitchen paper.

Using a teaspoon, fill the cannelloni tubes with the chicken and mushroom mixture. Transfer them to the dish. Pour the Béchamel Sauce over them to cover completely and sprinkle with the grated Parmesan cheese.

Bake in the preheated oven for 30 minutes, or until golden brown and bubbling. Serve immediately.

VARIATION
If you like, replace the Marsala with the same quantity of brandy and substitute the canned tomatoes with the same amount of fresh tomatoes.

serves 4 | prep 20 mins | cook 1hr 5 mins

vegetarian lasagne

This variation on the traditional meat-filled lasagne will appeal to vegetarians and meat-eaters alike.

INGREDIENTS
olive oil, for brushing
2 aubergines, sliced
2 tbsp butter
1 garlic clove, finely chopped
4 courgettes, sliced
1 tbsp finely chopped fresh
   flat-leaved parsley
1 tbsp finely chopped fresh marjoram
225 g/8 oz mozzarella cheese, grated
600 ml/1 pint passata
175 g/6 oz dried no-precook lasagne
600 ml/1 pint Béchamel Sauce
   (see page 27)
85 g/3 oz freshly grated Parmesan cheese
salt and pepper

Preheat the oven to 200°C/400°F/Gas Mark 6. Brush a large oven-proof dish with olive oil. Brush a large griddle pan with olive oil and heat until smoking. Add half the aubergine slices and cook over a medium heat for 8 minutes, or until golden brown all over. Remove the aubergine slices from the griddle pan and drain on kitchen paper. Add the remaining aubergine slices and extra oil, if necessary, and cook for 8 minutes, or until golden brown all over.

Melt the butter in a frying pan and add the garlic, courgettes, parsley and marjoram. Cook over a medium heat, stirring frequently, for 5 minutes, or until the courgettes are golden brown all over. Remove from the frying pan and drain on kitchen paper.

Layer the aubergine, courgettes, mozzarella, passata and lasagne in the dish, seasoning with salt and pepper as you go and finishing with a layer of lasagne. Pour over the Béchamel Sauce, making sure that all the pasta is covered. Sprinkle with the grated Parmesan cheese and bake in the preheated oven for 30–40 minutes, or until golden brown. Serve the lasagne immediately.

COOK'S TIP
Make sure that the oiled griddle pan is very hot before adding the aubergine slices. Add extra oil if the aubergine is sticking to the pan.

serves 4 | prep 15 mins | cook 40 mins

baked pasta with mushrooms

A bake of pasta, béchamel sauce, and a tasty filling is sometimes called a crostata.

INGREDIENTS
140 g/5 oz fontina cheese, thinly sliced
350 ml/12 fl oz hot Béchamel Sauce
  (see page 27)
6 tbsp butter, plus extra for greasing
350 g/12 oz mixed wild mushrooms, sliced
350 g/12 oz dried tagliatelle
2 egg yolks
4 tbsp freshly grated pecorino cheese
salt and pepper
mixed salad leaves, to serve

Preheat the oven to 200°C/400°F/Gas Mark 6. Stir the fontina cheese into the Béchamel Sauce and reserve.

Melt 2 tablespoons of butter in a large saucepan. Add the mushrooms and cook over a low heat, stirring, for 10 minutes.

Meanwhile, bring a large saucepan of lightly salted water to the boil. Add the pasta, return to the boil and cook for 8–10 minutes, or until the pasta is tender but still 'al dente'. Drain, return to the saucepan, and add the remaining butter, the egg yolks and about one-third of the sauce, then season to taste with salt and pepper. Toss well to mix, then gently stir in the mushrooms.

Lightly grease a large ovenproof dish with butter and spoon in the pasta mixture. Pour over the remaining sauce evenly and sprinkle with the grated pecorino cheese. Bake in the preheated oven for 15–20 minutes, or until golden brown. Serve immediately with mixed salad leaves.

serves 4 | prep 15 mins | cook 1hr 15 mins

sicilian spaghetti cake

This delicious classic dish of aubergines, tomatoes, meat and olives is perfect for both a family midweek supper or a special occasion main course. Serve with a fresh green salad.

INGREDIENTS
125 ml/4 fl oz olive oil, plus extra
    for greasing
2 aubergines, sliced
350 g/12 oz minced beef
1 onion, chopped
2 garlic cloves, chopped finely
2 tbsp tomato purée
400 g/14 oz canned chopped tomatoes
1 tsp Worcestershire sauce
1 tbsp chopped fresh
    flat-leaved parsley
10 stoned black olives, sliced
1 red pepper, deseeded and chopped
175 g/6 oz dried spaghetti
140 g/5 oz freshly grated
    Parmesan cheese
salt and pepper

Preheat the oven to 200°C/400°F/Gas Mark 6. Brush a 20-cm/ 8-inch loose-based round cake tin with oil and line the bottom with baking paper. Heat half the oil in a frying pan. Add the aubergines in batches, and cook until lightly browned on both sides. Add more oil, as required. Drain the aubergines on kitchen paper, then arrange in overlapping slices to cover the bottom and sides of the cake tin, reserving a few slices.

Heat the remaining olive oil in a large saucepan and add the beef, onion and garlic. Cook over a medium heat, breaking up the meat with a wooden spoon, until browned all over. Add the tomato purée, tomatoes and their can juices, Worcestershire sauce and parsley. Season to taste with salt and pepper and let simmer for 10 minutes. Add the olives and pepper and cook for 10 minutes.

Meanwhile, bring a saucepan of lightly salted water to the boil. Add the pasta, return to the boil and cook for 8–10 minutes, or until the pasta is tender but still 'al dente'. Drain and transfer to a bowl. Add the meat sauce and cheese and toss, then spoon into the cake tin, press down and cover with the remaining aubergine slices. Bake for 40 minutes. Leave the cake to stand for 5 minutes, then loosen round the edges and invert onto a plate. Remove and discard the baking paper and serve.

VARIATION
Other types of long pasta, such as linguine, also work well in this dish. Replace the red pepper with a yellow pepper, if you like.

serves 4 | prep 30 mins | cook 45 mins

seafood lasagne

You can use any type of white fish and any sauce you like in this recipe: try monkfish with whisky sauce or haddock with a cheese and parsley sauce.

INGREDIENTS
450 g/1 lb cod, filleted, skin
  removed and flesh flaked
115 g/4 oz peeled prawns
115 g/4 oz sole fillet, skin removed and
  flesh sliced
juice of 1 lemon
4 tbsp butter
3 leeks, very thinly sliced
60 g/2¼ oz plain flour
575 ml/18 fl oz milk
2 tbsp clear honey
240 g/8½ oz grated mozzarella cheese
450 g/1 lb no pre-cook lasagne
125 g/4½ oz freshly grated Parmesan cheese
pepper

VARIATION
For a cider sauce, substitute 1 finely chopped shallot for the leeks, 350 ml/12 fl oz cider and 350 ml/ 12 fl oz double cream for the milk, and 1 teaspoon of mustard for the honey. For a Tuscan sauce, substitute 1 fennel bulb for the leeks and omit the honey.

Preheat the oven to 180°C/350°/Gas Mark 4. Put the cod fillet, prawns and sole fillet into a large bowl and season with pepper and lemon juice according to taste. Set aside while you make the sauce.

Melt the butter in a large saucepan. Add the leeks and cook over a low heat, stirring occasionally, for about 8 minutes until soft. Add the flour and cook, stirring constantly, for 1 minute. Gradually stir in enough milk to make a thick, creamy sauce.

Blend in the honey and mozzarella and cook for a further 3 minutes. Remove the saucepan from the heat and mix in the fish and prawns.

Make alternate layers of fish sauce and lasagne in an ovenproof dish, finishing with a layer of fish sauce on top. Generously sprinkle over the grated Parmesan cheese and bake in the preheated oven for 30 minutes. Serve immediately.

serves 4 | prep 10 mins | cook 1hr 5 mins

traditional cannelloni

More delicately flavoured than the usual beef-filled cannelloni, this is still a substantial dish for a family supper.

INGREDIENTS
2 tbsp olive oil
2 onions, chopped
2 garlic cloves, finely chopped
1 tbsp shredded fresh basil
800 g/1 lb 12 oz canned
   chopped tomatoes
1 tbsp tomato purée
350 g/12 oz dried cannelloni tubes
butter, for greasing
140 g/5 oz ricotta cheese
115 g/4 oz cooked ham, diced
1 egg
70 g/2½ oz freshly grated
   pecorino cheese
salt and pepper

Preheat the oven to 180°C/350°F/Gas Mark 4. Heat the olive oil in a large heavy-based frying pan. Add the onions and garlic and cook over a low heat, stirring occasionally, for 5 minutes, or until the onion is softened. Add the basil, chopped tomatoes and their can juices, and tomato purée, and season to taste with salt and pepper. Reduce the heat and simmer for 30 minutes, or until thickened.

Meanwhile, bring a large heavy-based saucepan of lightly salted water to the boil. Add the cannelloni tubes, return to the boil, and cook for 8–10 minutes, or until tender but still 'al dente'. Using a slotted spoon, transfer the cannelloni tubes to a large plate and pat dry with kitchen paper.

Grease a large, shallow ovenproof dish with butter. Mix the ricotta, ham and egg together in a bowl and season to taste with salt and pepper. Using a teaspoon, fill the cannelloni tubes with the ricotta mixture and place in a single layer in the dish. Pour the tomato sauce over the cannelloni and sprinkle with the grated pecorino cheese. Bake in the preheated oven for 30 minutes, or until golden brown. Serve immediately.

VARIATION
Substitute the pecorino cheese with the same amount of freshly grated Parmesan cheese, if you prefer.

serves 4 | prep 1hr 15 mins | cook 25 mins

tortelloni

These tasty little squares of pasta stuffed with mushrooms and cheese are surprisingly filling. This recipe makes 36 tortelloni.

INGREDIENTS
300 g/10½ oz Basic Pasta Dough
  (see page 25), rolled out to thin sheets
75 g/2¾ oz butter
50 g/1¾ oz shallots, finely chopped
3 garlic cloves, crushed
50 g/1¾ oz mushrooms, wiped and
  chopped finely
½ stick celery, finely chopped
25 g/1 oz pecorino cheese, finely grated,
  plus extra to garnish
1 tbsp oil
salt and pepper

Using a serrated pasta cutter, cut 5-cm/2-inch squares from the sheets of fresh pasta. To make 36 tortelloni you will need 72 squares. Once the pasta is cut, cover the squares with clingfilm to stop them drying out.

Heat 40 g/1½ oz butter in a frying pan. Add the shallots, 1 crushed garlic clove, the mushrooms and the celery and cook for 4–5 minutes.

Remove the frying pan from the heat, stir in the cheese and season with salt and pepper to taste.

Spoon ½ teaspoon of the mixture onto the middle of 36 pasta squares. Brush the edges of the squares with water and top with the remaining 36 squares. Press the edges together to seal. Leave to rest for at least 5 minutes.

Bring a large saucepan of water to the boil, add the oil and cook the tortelloni, in batches, for 2–3 minutes. The tortelloni will rise to the surface when cooked and the pasta should be tender but still 'al dente'. Remove from the saucepan with a slotted spoon and drain thoroughly.

Meanwhile, melt the remaining butter in a saucepan. Add the remaining garlic and plenty of pepper and cook for 1–2 minutes. Transfer the tortelloni to serving plates and pour over the garlic butter. Garnish with grated pecorino cheese and serve.

serves 4 | prep 25 mins | cook 50 mins

green easter pie

*This traditional Easter risotto pie is from
Piedmont in northern Italy.
Serve it warm or chilled in slices.*

INGREDIENTS
2 tbsp olive oil, plus extra for greasing
85 g/3 oz rocket
1 onion, chopped
2 garlic cloves, chopped
200 g/7 oz risotto rice
700 ml/1¼ pints hot Chicken Stock or
    Vegetable Stock (see page 29)
125 ml/4 fl oz white wine
50 g/1¾ oz Parmesan cheese, grated
100 g/3½ oz frozen peas, defrosted
2 tomatoes, diced
4 eggs, beaten
3 tbsp fresh marjoram, chopped
50 g/1¾ oz breadcrumbs
salt and pepper

Preheat the oven to 180°C/350°F/Gas Mark
4. Lightly grease and then line the base of
a 23-cm/9-inch deep cake tin.

Using a sharp knife, roughly chop the rocket
and set aside.

Heat the oil in a large frying pan. Add the
onion and garlic and cook for 4–5 minutes
or until soft.

Add the rice to the mixture in the frying
pan, mix well to combine, then begin
adding the stock a ladleful at a time. Wait
until all of the stock has been absorbed
before adding another ladleful of liquid.

Continue to cook the mixture, adding the
wine, until the rice is tender. This will take
at least 15 minutes.

Stir in the Parmesan cheese, peas, rocket,
tomatoes, eggs and 2 tablespoons of
the marjoram. Season to taste with salt
and pepper.

Spoon the risotto into the frying pan and
level the surface by pressing down with the
back of a wooden spoon.

Top with the breadcrumbs and the
remaining marjoram and bake in the
preheated oven for 30 minutes. Cut the
pie into slices and serve immediately.

serves 6 | prep 10 mins + 30 mins soaking | cook 40 mins

sunshine risotto

Pecorino is an Italian cheese made from sheep's milk. Although it is made all over Italy, the aged pecorino from Sardinia is particularly fine.

INGREDIENTS
about 12 sun-dried tomatoes
generous 1.5 litres/2¾ pints
   Chicken or Vegetable Stock
   (see page 29)
2 tbsp olive oil
1 large onion,
   finely chopped
4-6 garlic cloves,
   finely chopped
400g/14 oz risotto rice
2 tbsp chopped fresh
   flat-leaved parsley
85 g/3 oz freshly grated
   aged pecorino cheese
extra virgin olive oil,
   for drizzling

Place the sun-dried tomatoes in an ovenproof bowl and pour over enough boiling water to cover. Set aside to soak for 30 minutes, or until soft and supple. Drain and pat dry with kitchen paper, shred thinly and set aside.

Bring the stock to the boil in a saucepan, then reduce the heat and keep simmering gently over a low heat until you are ready to add it to the risotto.

Heat the olive oil in a deep saucepan over a medium heat. Add the onion and cook, stirring occasionally, for 2 minutes, or until starting to soften. Add the garlic and cook for an additional 15 seconds.

Reduce the heat, add the rice and mix to coat in oil. Cook, stirring constantly, for 2–3 minutes, or until the grains are translucent.

Gradually add the hot stock, a ladleful at a time. Stir constantly, adding more liquid as the rice absorbs each addition. Increase the heat to medium so that the liquid bubbles. After approximately 15 minutes, stir in the sun-dried tomatoes.

Continue adding the stock, stirring constantly, until the risotto has been cooking for 20 minutes, or until all the liquid is absorbed and the rice is creamy.

Remove the pan from the heat and stir in the chopped parsley and half the pecorino cheese. Spoon the risotto onto six warmed plates. Drizzle with extra virgin olive oil and sprinkle the remaining pecorino cheese on top. Serve at once.

serves 4 | prep 15 mins | cook 30 mins

blue cheese risotto

One of the world's oldest veined cheeses, Gorgonzola is a rich creamy colour with delicate green veining, although it is always known as a blue cheese. It has a piquant but subtly rich flavour and an appetizing aroma. If it smells bitter, or the texture feels hard and dry, do not buy it. Dolcelatte is a creamier, milder version of Gorgonzola created during the 1960s.

INGREDIENTS
1.2 litres/2 pints Vegetable Stock
   (see page 29)
1 tbsp olive oil
40 g/1½ oz butter
1 small onion,
   finely chopped
55 g/2 oz rindless bacon slices, diced
280 g/10 oz risotto rice
115 g/4 oz Gorgonzola or dolcelatte cheese
salt and pepper

Bring the stock to the boil in a saucepan, reduce the heat and simmer gently over a low heat while you are cooking the risotto.

Heat the oil with 25 g/1 oz of the butter in a deep saucepan over a low heat until the butter has melted. Stir in the onion and bacon and cook, stirring occasionally, for 5 minutes, or until the bacon is just starting to brown and the onion is soft.

Add the rice and mix to coat in oil and butter. Cook, stirring constantly, for 2–3 minutes, or until the grains are translucent.

Gradually add the hot stock, a ladleful at a time. Stir constantly and add more liquid as the rice absorbs each addition. Increase the heat to medium so that the liquid bubbles. Cook for 20 minutes, or until all the liquid is absorbed and the rice is creamy. Season to taste with salt and pepper.

Remove the risotto from the heat and add the remaining butter. Mix well, then crumble in half the blue cheese and stir well until it melts. Season well with plenty of pepper.

Spoon the risotto onto warmed plates. Crumble or dice the remaining blue cheese and sprinkle it over the top of the risotto before serving.

serves 4 | prep 15 mins | cook 35 mins

crunchy walnut risotto

Risotti, like soufflés, should not be kept waiting while your guests come to the table. Once the 'mantecatura' – the final addition, usually butter and grated Parmesan – has been beaten in to make the texture even creamier, the risotto should be served.

INGREDIENTS
1.2 litres/2 pints Vegetable Stock
  (see page 29)
1 tbsp olive oil
70 g/2½ oz butter
1 small onion, finely chopped
280 g/10 oz risotto rice
115 g/4 oz walnut halves
85 g/3 oz freshly grated Parmesan or
  Grana Padano cheese
55 g/2 oz mascarpone cheese
55 g/2 oz Gorgonzola
  cheese, diced
salt and pepper

Bring the stock to the boil in a saucepan, reduce the heat and simmer gently over a low heat while you are cooking the risotto.

Heat the oil with 25 g/1 oz of the butter in a deep saucepan over a medium heat until the butter has melted. Add the onion and cook, stirring occasionally, for 5–7 minutes, or until soft and starting to turn golden. Do not brown.

Reduce the heat, add the rice and mix to coat in oil and butter. Cook, stirring constantly, for 2–3 minutes, or until the grains are translucent.

Gradually add the hot stock, a ladleful at a time. Stir constantly and add more liquid as the rice absorbs each addition. Increase the heat to medium so that the liquid bubbles. Cook for 20 minutes, or until all the liquid is absorbed and the rice is creamy. Season to taste with salt and pepper.

While the risotto is cooking, melt 25 g/1 oz of the remaining butter in a frying pan over a medium heat. Add the walnuts and toss for 2–3 minutes, or until just starting to brown.

Remove the risotto from the heat and add the remaining butter. Mix well, then stir in the Parmesan, mascarpone and Gorgonzola cheeses until they melt, along with most of the walnuts. Spoon the risotto onto warmed plates, sprinkle with the remaining walnuts and serve.

serves 6 | prep 15 mins | cook 35 mins

minted green risotto

This tasty risotto gets its vibrant green colour from the spinach and mint. Serve with Italian-style rustic bread and salad for an informal supper.

INGREDIENTS
1 litre/1¾ pints Chicken or Vegetable Stock (see page 29)
25 g/1 oz butter
225 g/8 oz shelled fresh peas or thawed frozen peas
250 g/9 oz fresh young spinach leaves, washed and drained
1 bunch of fresh mint, leaves stripped from stalks
2 tbsp chopped fresh basil
2 tbsp chopped fresh oregano
pinch of freshly grated nutmeg
4 tbsp mascarpone cheese or double cream
2 tbsp vegetable oil
1 onion, finely chopped
2 celery sticks, including leaves, finely chopped
2 garlic cloves, finely chopped
½ tsp dried thyme
300 g/10½ oz risotto rice
50 ml/2 fl oz dry white vermouth
85 g/3 oz freshly grated Parmesan cheese

Bring the stock to the boil in a saucepan, reduce the heat and simmer gently over a low heat while you are cooking the risotto.

Heat half the butter in a deep frying pan over a medium-high heat until sizzling. Add the peas, spinach, mint leaves, basil and oregano and season with the nutmeg. Cook, stirring frequently, for 3 minutes, or until the spinach and mint leaves are wilted. Cool slightly.

Pour the spinach mixture into a food processor and process for 15 seconds. Add the mascarpone and process again for 1 minute. Transfer to a bowl and set aside.

Heat the oil and remaining butter in a large, heavy-based saucepan over a medium heat. Add the onion, celery, garlic and thyme and cook, stirring occasionally, for 2 minutes, or until the vegetables are softened.

Reduce the heat, add the rice and mix to coat in oil and butter. Cook, stirring constantly, for 2–3 minutes, or until the grains are translucent. Add the vermouth and cook, stirring constantly, until it has reduced.

Gradually add the hot stock, a ladleful at a time. Stir constantly and add more liquid as the rice absorbs each addition. Increase the heat to medium so that the liquid bubbles. Cook for 20 minutes, or until the liquid is absorbed and the rice is creamy.

Stir in the spinach-mascarpone mixture and the Parmesan. Transfer to warmed plates and serve at once.

VARIATION
If you don't have any vermouth, you can substitute the same quantity of dry white wine.

serves 4 | prep 15 mins | cook 35 mins

rice & peas

This famous and rather pretty dish is one of many risotti from the Veneto.

INGREDIENTS
1 litre/1¾ pints Vegetable Stock
  (see page 29)
85 g/3 oz butter
3 shallots, chopped finely
115 g/4 oz pancetta, diced
280 g/10 oz risotto rice
150 ml/5 fl oz dry white wine
225 g/8 oz petits pois, thawed if using frozen
salt and pepper
Parmesan cheese shavings, to garnish

Bring the stock to the boil in a large saucepan, reduce the heat and simmer gently while you are cooking the risotto.

Melt 55 g/2 oz butter in another large, heavy-based saucepan. Add the shallots and pancetta and cook over a low heat, stirring occasionally, for 5 minutes, until the shallots are softened. Add the rice and cook, stirring constantly, for 2–3 minutes, until all the grains are thoroughly coated and glistening.

Pour in the wine and cook, stirring constantly, until it has almost completely evaporated. Add a ladleful of hot stock and cook, stirring constantly, until all the stock has been absorbed. Continue cooking and adding the stock, a ladleful at a time, for about 10 minutes.

Add the peas, then continue adding the stock, a ladleful at a time, for an additional 10 minutes, or until the rice is tender and the liquid has been absorbed.

Stir in the remaining butter and season to taste with salt and pepper. Transfer to a warmed serving dish, garnish with Parmesan shavings and serve immediately.

VARIATION
You can substitute diced cooked ham for the pancetta and add it towards the end of the cooking time so that it heats through.

serves 2 | prep 20 mins | cook 1 hr

rice-filled aubergines

An aubergine is halved and filled with a risotto mixture, topped with cheese, and then baked to make a snack or quick meal for two.

INGREDIENTS
60 g/2¼ oz mixed long-grain
   and wild rice
1 aubergine, about 350 g/12 oz
1 tbsp olive oil
1 small onion, finely chopped
1 garlic clove, crushed
½ small red pepper, cored, deseeded
   and chopped
2 tbsp water
25 g/1 oz raisins
25 g/1 oz cashew nuts,
   chopped roughly
½ tsp dried oregano
40 g/1½ oz Cheddar or Parmesan cheese,
   grated
salt and pepper
fresh parsley, to garnish

Preheat the oven to 190°C/375°F/Gas Mark 5. Bring a saucepan of lightly salted water the the boil, add the rice, return to the boil and cook for 15 minutes or until the rice is tender. Drain, rinse and drain again.

Bring a large saucepan of water to the boil. Cut the stem off the aubergine and then cut in half lengthways. Cut out the flesh from the centre, leaving a 1.5-cm/½-inch shell. Blanch the shells in the boiling water for 3–4 minutes. Drain, then finely chop.

Heat the oil in a frying pan, add the onion and garlic and fry over a low heat until just beginning to soften. Add the pepper and aubergine flesh and cook for 2 minutes. Add the water and cook for 2–3 minutes.

Stir the raisins, cashew nuts, oregano and rice into the aubergine mixture and season to taste with salt and pepper.

Lay the aubergine shells in an ovenproof dish and spoon in the rice mixture, piling it up well. Cover and bake in the preheated oven for 20 minutes.

Remove the dish from the oven, take off the lid and sprinkle the cheese over the rice. Place under a preheated moderate grill for 3–4 minutes. Serve hot, garnished with parsley.

serves 4 | prep 15 mins | cook 35 mins

chicken risotto with saffron

*The possibilities for this risotto are endless
– try adding the following just at the end
of the cooking time: cashew nuts and
corn, lightly sautéed courgettes and basil,
or artichokes and oyster mushrooms.*

INGREDIENTS
1.3 litres/2¼ pints Chicken Stock
  (see page 29)
125 g/4½ oz butter
900 g/2 lb skinless, boneless chicken
  breasts, thinly sliced
1 large onion, chopped
500 g/1 lb 2 oz risotto rice
150 ml/5 fl oz white wine
1 tsp crumbled saffron threads
55 g/2 oz freshly grated Parmesan cheese
salt and pepper

Bring the stock to the boil in a saucepan,
reduce the heat and simmer gently over a
low heat while you are cooking the risotto.

Meanwhile, heat 55 g/2 oz of the butter
in a deep saucepan, add the chicken and
onion and cook, stirring frequently, for
8 minutes, or until golden brown.

Add the rice and mix to coat in the butter.
Cook, stirring constantly for 2–3 minutes,
or until the grains are translucent. Add
the wine and cook, stirring constantly, for
1 minute until reduced.

Mix the saffron with 4 tablespoons of the
hot stock. Add the liquid to the rice and
cook, stirring constantly, until it is absorbed.

Gradually add the remaining hot stock,
a ladleful at a time. Stir constantly and
add more liquid as the rice absorbs each
addition. Cook for 20 minutes, or until all
the liquid is absorbed and the rice is
creamy. Season to taste.

Remove the risotto from the heat and
add the remaining butter. Mix well, then
stir in the Parmesan until it melts. Spoon
the risotto onto warmed plates and serve
immediately.

serves 4 | prep 15 mins | cook 35 mins

shredded spinach & ham risotto

For a spicier flavour, you could substitute salami for the ham. Make sure that you peel off any rind before cutting the slices into strips.

INGREDIENTS
225 g/8 oz fresh young spinach leaves
115 g/4 oz cooked ham
1 litre/1¾ pints Chicken Stock
  (see page 29)
1 tbsp olive oil
40 g/1½ oz butter
1 small onion, finely chopped
280 g/10 oz risotto rice
150 ml/5 fl oz dry white wine
50 ml/2 fl oz single cream
85 g/3 oz freshly grated Parmesan or
  Grana Padano cheese
salt and pepper

Wash the spinach well and slice into thin shreds. Cut the ham into thin strips.

Bring the stock to the boil in a saucepan, reduce the heat and simmer gently over a low heat while you are cooking the risotto.

Heat the oil with 25 g/1 oz butter in a deep saucepan over a medium heat until the butter has melted. Add the onion and cook, stirring occasionally, for 5 minutes, or until soft and starting to turn golden. Do not brown.

Reduce the heat, add the rice and mix to coat in oil and butter. Cook, stirring constantly, for 2–3 minutes, or until the grains are translucent.

Add the wine and cook, stirring constantly, for 1 minute until reduced.

Gradually add the hot stock, a ladleful at a time. Stir constantly and add more liquid as the rice absorbs each addition. Increase the heat to medium so that the liquid bubbles. Cook for 20 minutes, or until all the liquid is absorbed and the rice is creamy. Add the spinach and ham with the last ladleful of stock.

Remove the risotto from the heat and add the remaining butter and the cream. Mix well, then stir in the Parmesan until it melts. Season to taste and serve immediately.

serves 4 | prep 1hr 15 mins + 1 hr chilling | cook 45 mins

gnocchi romana

This is a traditional Italian recipe but, for a less rich version, simply omit the eggs.

INGREDIENTS
700 ml/1¼ pints milk
pinch of freshly grated nutmeg
90 g/3¼ oz butter, plus extra
  for greasing
225 g/8 oz semolina
125 g/4½ oz grated
  Parmesan cheese
2 eggs, beaten
60 g/2¼ oz grated Gruyère cheese
salt and pepper
fresh basil sprigs, to garnish

Pour the milk into a saucepan and bring to the boil. Remove the pan from the heat and stir in the nutmeg, 2 tablespoons of butter and salt and pepper.

Gradually stir the semolina into the milk, whisking to prevent lumps forming, and return the saucepan to a low heat. Simmer, stirring constantly, for about 10 minutes, or until very thick.

Beat 100g/3½ oz of the Parmesan cheese into the semolina mixture, then beat in the eggs. Continue beating the mixture until smooth. Set the mixture aside for a few minutes to cool slightly.

Spread out the cooled semolina mixture in an even layer on a sheet of baking paper or on a large, oiled baking sheet, smoothing the surface with a damp spatula – it should be 1 cm/½ inch thick. Set aside to cool completely, then chill in the refrigerator for 1 hour.

Once chilled, cut out rounds of gnocchi, measuring about 4 cm/1½ inches in diameter, using a plain, greased pastry cutter.

Preheat the oven to 200°C/400°F/Gas Mark 6. Grease a shallow ovenproof dish or four individual dishes. Lay the gnocchi trimmings in the base of the dish or dishes and cover with overlapping rounds of gnocchi.

Melt the remaining butter and drizzle over the gnocchi. Sprinkle over the remaining Parmesan cheese, then sprinkle over the Gruyère cheese.

Bake in the preheated oven for 25–30 minutes, until the top is crisp and golden brown. Serve hot, garnished with the basil sprigs.

serves 4 | prep 30 mins + 1 hr chilling | cook 15 mins

spinach & ricotta gnocchi

These mouthwatering dumplings, made with spinach and ricotta cheese are best served simply, coated in a herb butter and sprinkled with Parmesan cheese.

INGREDIENTS
1 kg/2 lb 4 oz fresh spinach, coarse stalks removed
350 g/12 oz ricotta cheese
115 g/4 oz freshly grated Parmesan cheese
3 eggs, lightly beaten
pinch of freshly grated nutmeg
115–175 g/4–6 oz plain flour, plus extra for dusting
salt and pepper

herb butter
115 g/4 oz unsalted butter
2 tbsp chopped fresh oregano
2 tbsp chopped fresh sage

Wash the spinach, and place it in a saucepan. Cover and cook over a low heat for 6–8 minutes, until just wilted. Drain well and set aside to cool.

Squeeze or press out as much liquid as possible from the spinach, then chop finely or process in a food processor or blender. Place the spinach in a bowl and add the ricotta, half the Parmesan, the eggs and nutmeg, and season to taste with salt and pepper. Beat until thoroughly combined. Start by sifting in 115 g/4 oz of the flour and lightly work it into the mixture, adding more, if necessary, to make a workable mixture. Cover with clingfilm and chill for 1 hour.

With floured hands, break off small pieces of the mixture and roll them into walnut-sized balls. Handle them as little as possible, as they are quite delicate. Lightly dust the dumplings with flour.

Bring a large saucepan of lightly salted water to the boil. Add the dumplings and cook for 2–3 minutes, until they rise to the surface. Remove from the saucepan with a slotted spoon, drain well and set aside.

Meanwhile, make the herb butter. Melt the butter in a heavy-based frying pan. Add the oregano and sage and cook over a low heat, stirring frequently, for 1 minute. Add the dumplings, toss for 1 minute to coat, transfer to a warm serving dish, sprinkle with the remaining Parmesan and serve.

serves 4 | prep 30 mins + 1 hr chilling | cook 40 mins

basil gnocchi

*While gnocchi are traditionally served
in Italy as a primo or first course, they
can also make an unusual and delicious
accompaniment to meat or fish.*

INGREDIENTS
700 ml/1¼ pints milk
200 g/7 oz semolina
1 tbsp finely chopped fresh basil leaves
4 sun-dried tomatoes in oil, drained and
  finely chopped
2 eggs, lightly beaten
55 g/2 oz butter, plus extra for greasing
85 g/3 oz freshly grated Parmesan cheese
flour, for dusting
salt and pepper
Basic Tomato Sauce (see page 26), to serve

Pour the milk into a large saucepan and
bring to just below boiling point. Sprinkle in
the semolina, stirring constantly. Reduce
the heat and simmer gently for about
2 minutes, until thick and smooth. Remove
the saucepan from the heat.

Stir in the basil, sun-dried tomatoes, eggs,
half the butter and half the Parmesan, and
season to taste with salt and pepper. Stir
well until all the ingredients are thoroughly
incorporated, then pour into a shallow dish
or baking tray and level the surface.
Set aside to cool, then chill for at least
1 hour, until set.

Preheat the oven to 190°C/375°F/Gas Mark
5. Lightly grease an ovenproof dish with
butter. Using a lightly floured, plain round
cutter, stamp out circles of the set semolina
mixture. Place the trimmings in the base of
the dish and top with the circles.

Melt the remaining butter and brush it over
the semolina circles, then sprinkle with the
remaining Parmesan cheese. Bake in the
preheated oven for 30–35 minutes, until
golden. Serve immediately with Basic
Tomato Sauce.

part three

SECONDI PIATTI
meat, poultry, game, fish & seafood, vegetable main courses

The meat and poultry eaten in Italy is lean and tender, the seafood is fresh and so are the vegetables. With all these ingredients, it is the quality, not the quantity, that is the key to the main course in Italy, and the recipes in this chapter represent the very best of Italy's main courses.

serves 4 | prep 15 mins | cook 3 hrs 30 mins

beef in red wine

Apart from producing what is arguably the best olive oil in the world, Tuscany is renowned for producing quite simple dishes in which the flavours are perfectly harmonized. This is one of them.

INGREDIENTS
1.25 kg/2 lb 12 oz topside of beef
3 tbsp olive oil
1 red onion, chopped
1 garlic clove, chopped finely
2 carrots, sliced
2 celery sticks, sliced
300 ml/10 fl oz Chianti
200 g/7 oz canned tomatoes, chopped
1 tbsp chopped fresh oregano
1 tbsp chopped fresh flat-leaved parsley
1 bay leaf
salt and pepper

Preheat the oven to 180°C/350°F/ Gas Mark 4. Season the beef all over with salt and pepper. Heat the olive oil in a large, flameproof casserole. Add the beef and cook over a medium heat, turning frequently, until brown on all sides. Use 2 large forks to remove the beef from the casserole.

Reduce the heat, add the onion, garlic, carrots and celery, and cook, stirring occasionally, for 5 minutes, until soft. Pour in the wine and add the tomatoes, oregano, parsley and bay leaf. Stir well to mix and bring to the boil.

Return the meat to the casserole and spoon the vegetable mixture over it. Cover and cook in the preheated oven, spooning the vegetables over the meat occasionally, for 3–3¼ hours, until the beef is tender.

Transfer the beef to a carving board and cover with foil. Place the casserole on a high heat and bring the juices to the boil. Continue to boil until the juices have reduced and thickened.

Carve the beef into slices and place on a warmed serving platter. Strain the thickened cooking juices over the beef and serve immediately.

serves 4 | prep 10 mins | cook 26 mins

pizzaiola steak

Originating in Naples, where it is difficult to find any dish that does not feature the brilliantly coloured, rich-tasting tomatoes of the region, this way of serving steak is now popular throughout Italy and beyond.

COOK'S TIP
*To peel tomatoes, place them in a heatproof bowl, pour boiling water over them, and soak for 3–4 minutes. When cool enough to handle make a cross in the base of each tomato with a sharp knife – the skins will peel away easily.

INGREDIENTS
3 tbsp olive oil, plus extra for brushing
700 g/1 lb 9 oz tomatoes, peeled* and
   chopped
1 red pepper, deseeded and chopped
1 onion, chopped
2 garlic cloves, finely chopped
1 tbsp chopped fresh flat-leaved parsley
1 tsp dried oregano
1 tsp sugar
4 x 175 g/6 oz entrecôte or rump steaks
salt and pepper

Place the oil, tomatoes, red pepper, onion, garlic, parsley, oregano and sugar in a heavy-based saucepan and season to taste with salt and pepper. Bring to the boil, reduce the heat and simmer for 15 minutes.

Meanwhile, snip any fat round the outsides of the steaks. Season each generously with pepper (but no salt) and brush with olive oil. Cook on a very hot preheated griddle pan for 1 minute on each side. Reduce the heat to medium and cook according to taste: 1½–2 minutes each side for rare; 2½–3 minutes each side for medium; 3–4 minutes on each side for well done.

Transfer the steaks to warmed individual plates and spoon the sauce over them. Serve immediately.

serves 6 | prep 35 mins | cook 1 hr 30 mins

layered meat loaf

The hidden pasta layer comes as a pleasant surprise inside this lightly spiced meat loaf.

INGREDIENTS
25 g/1 oz butter, plus extra
   for greasing
1 small onion, finely chopped
1 small red pepper, cored, deseeded
   and chopped
1 garlic clove, chopped
450 g/1 lb minced beef
25 g/1 oz white breadcrumbs
½ tsp cayenne pepper
1 tbsp lemon juice
½ tsp grated lemon rind
2 tbsp chopped fresh parsley
90 g/3¼ oz dried short pasta,
   such as fusilli
1 tbsp olive oil
225 ml/8 fl oz Béchamel Sauce
   (see page 27)
4 bay leaves
175 g/6 oz streaky bacon, rinds removed
salt and pepper
salad leaves, to serve

Preheat the oven to 180°C/350°F/Gas Mark 4. Melt the butter in a frying pan over a medium heat, add the onion and red pepper and fry for about 3 minutes. Stir in the garlic and cook for 1 minute or until soft.

Put the meat into a bowl and mash with a wooden spoon until sticky. Add the onion mixture, breadcrumbs, cayenne pepper, lemon juice, lemon rind and parsley. Season and set aside.

Bring a saucepan of lightly salted water to the boil. Add the pasta and oil and cook for 8–10 minutes, until the pasta is almost tender. Drain and stir into the Béchamel Sauce.

Grease a 1-kg loaf/2 lb 4-oz loaf tin and arrange the bay leaves in the base. Stretch the bacon slices with the back of a knife and line the base and sides of the tin with them. Spoon in half the meat mixture and smooth the surface. Cover with the pasta mixed with Béchamel Sauce, then spoon in the remaining meat mixture. Level the top and cover with foil.

Bake in the preheated oven for 1 hour, or until the juices run clear when a skewer is inserted into the centre and the loaf has shrunk away from the sides. Pour off any fat and turn out the loaf onto a serving dish. Serve with salad leaves.

VARIATION
Add 2 tablespoons of grated Parmesan cheese to the Béchamel Sauce before adding the pasta.

serves 4 | prep 45 mins | cook 1 hr 45 mins

rich beef stew

This slow-cooked beef stew is flavoured with the flesh and rind of oranges, red wine and porcini mushrooms.

INGREDIENTS
1 tbsp oil
1 tbsp butter
225 g/8 oz baby onions, peeled and halved
600 g/1 lb 5 oz stewing steak, diced into
   4-cm/1½-inch chunks
300 ml/10 fl oz beef stock
150 ml/5 fl oz red wine
4 tbsp chopped oregano
1 tbsp sugar
1 orange
25 g/1 oz porcini or other dried mushrooms
225 g/8 oz fresh plum tomatoes
cooked rice or potatoes, to serve

Preheat the oven to 180°C/350°F/Gas Mark 4. Heat the oil and butter in a large frying pan. Add the onions and sauté for 5 minutes or until golden. Remove the onions with a slotted spoon, set aside and keep warm.

Add the beef to the pan and cook, stirring, for 5 minutes, or until brown all over.

Return the onions to the pan and add the stock, wine, oregano and sugar, stirring to mix well. Transfer the mixture to an ovenproof casserole dish.

Pare the rind from the orange and cut it into strips. Slice the orange flesh into rings. Add the orange rings and the rind to the casserole and cook in the preheated oven for 1¼ hours.

Soak the porcini mushrooms for 30 minutes in a small bowl containing 4 tablespoons of warm water.

Peel and halve the tomatoes (see Cook's Tip, page 111). Add the tomatoes, mushrooms and their soaking liquid to the casserole. Cook for a further 20 minutes until the beef is tender and the juices are thickened. Serve with cooked rice.

COOK'S TIP
If fresh plum tomatoes are unavailable use the canned whole variety rather than another variety of fresh tomato.

serves 4 | prep 30 mins + 1 hr chilling | cook 6 mins

pan-fried pork with mozzarella

Although many cities are snapping at the Eternal City's heels for the title of gastronomic capital of Italy, Rome still wears the crown, as this Roman dish demonstrates.

INGREDIENTS
450 g/1 lb loin of pork
2–3 garlic cloves, finely chopped
175 g/6 oz mozzarella cheese, drained
12 slices prosciutto
12 fresh sage leaves
55 g/2 oz unsalted butter
salt and pepper
mostarda di Verona,* to serve (optional)
flat-leaved parsley sprigs and lemon slices,
  to garnish

Trim any excess fat from the meat, then slice it crossways into 12 pieces, each about 2.5 cm/1 inch thick. Stand each piece on end and beat with the flat end of a meat mallet or the side of a rolling pin until thoroughly flattened. Rub each piece all over with garlic, transfer to a plate and cover with clingfilm. Set aside in a cool place for 30 minutes to 1 hour.

Cut the mozzarella into 12 slices. Season the pork to taste with salt and pepper, then place a slice of cheese on top of each slice of meat. Top with a slice of prosciutto, letting it fall in folds. Place a sage leaf on each portion. Secure with a cocktail stick.

Melt the butter in a large, heavy-based frying pan. Add the pork, in batches if necessary, and cook for 2–3 minutes on each side, until the meat is tender and the cheese has melted. Remove with a slotted spoon and keep warm while you cook the remaining batch.

Transfer the pork to 4 warmed individual plates, garnish with parsley and lemon slices and serve immediately with mostarda di Verona, if using.

COOK'S TIP
Mostarda di Verona is made with apple purée and is available from some good Italian delicatessens.

serves 4 | prep 20 mins | cook 12 mins

pork fillets with fennel

This is a very rich dish with a creamy Gorgonzola sauce that provides a perfect balance for the aniseed flavour of the fennel and the Italian liqueur, Sambuca.

INGREDIENTS
450 g/1 lb pork fillet
2–3 tbsp virgin olive oil
2 tbsp Sambuca liqueur
1 large fennel bulb, sliced
85 g/3 oz Gorgonzola cheese, crumbled
2 tbsp single cream
1 tbsp chopped fresh sage
1 tbsp chopped fresh thyme
salt and pepper

Trim any fat from the pork and cut into 5-mm/¼-inch thick slices. Place the slices between 2 sheets of clingfilm and beat with the flat end of a meat mallet or with a rolling pin to flatten slightly.

Heat 2 tablespoons of the oil in a heavy-based frying pan and add the pork, in batches. Cook over a medium heat for 2–3 minutes on each side, until tender. Remove from the frying pan and keep warm. Cook the remaining batches, adding more oil if necessary.

Stir the Sambuca into the frying pan, increase the heat and cook, stirring constantly and scraping up the glazed bits from the bottom. Add the fennel and cook, stirring and turning frequently, for 3 minutes. Remove the fennel from the frying pan and keep warm.

Reduce the heat, add the Gorgonzola and cream and cook, stirring constantly, until smooth. Remove the frying pan from the heat, stir in the sage and thyme and season to taste with salt and pepper.

Divide the pork and fennel between four warmed serving plates, pour over the sauce and serve immediately.

serves 4 | prep 25 mins | cook 1 hr

pork with lemon & garlic

This is a simplified version of a traditional dish from the Marche region of Italy. Pork fillet pockets are stuffed with prosciutto and herbs.

INGREDIENTS
450 g/1 lb pork fillet
50 g/1¾ oz chopped almonds
2 tbsp olive oil
100 g/3½ oz raw prosciutto di Parma,
   finely chopped
2 garlic cloves, chopped
1 tbsp fresh oregano, chopped
finely grated rind of 2 lemons
4 shallots, finely chopped
175 ml/6 fl oz Chicken Stock (see page 29)
1 tsp sugar

Using a sharp knife, cut the pork fillet into four equal pieces. Place the pork between sheets of waxed paper and pound each piece with a meat mallet or the end of a rolling pin to flatten it.

Cut a horizontal slit in each piece of pork to make a pocket.

Place the almonds on a baking tray. Lightly toast the almonds under a medium-hot grill for 2–3 minutes or until golden.

Mix the almonds with 1 tablespoon oil, the prosciutto, garlic, oregano and the finely grated rind of 1 lemon. Spoon the mixture into the pockets of the pork.

Heat the remaining oil in a large frying pan. Add the shallots and cook for 2 minutes or until soft.

Add the pork to the frying pan and cook for 2 minutes on each side or until the pork is browned all over.

Add the stock to the frying pan, bring to the boil, cover and simmer for 45 minutes or until the pork is tender. Remove the meat from the frying pan, set aside and keep warm.

Add the remaining lemon rind and sugar to the pan and boil for 3–4 minutes or until reduced and syrupy. Pour the lemon sauce over the pork fillets and serve immediately.

serves 6 | prep 25 mins | cook 2 hrs 45 mins

slow-roasted pork

This wonderfully succulent roast from Perugia may be served hot with French beans or peperonata or cold with a crisp green salad.

COOK'S TIP
Ready-prepared boned and rolled loin of pork is available from supermarkets and butchers, or you can ask your butcher to prepare one for you.

INGREDIENTS
1.6 kg/3 lb 8 oz loin of pork,
  boned and rolled*
4 garlic cloves, sliced thinly lengthways
1½ tsp finely chopped fresh fennel fronds
  or ½ tsp dried fennel
4 cloves
300 ml/10 fl oz dry white wine
300 ml/10 fl oz water
salt and pepper

Preheat the oven to 150°C/300°F/ Gas Mark 2. Use a small, sharp knife to make incisions all over the pork, opening them out slightly to make little pockets. Place the garlic slices in a small sieve and rinse under cold running water to moisten. Spread out the fennel on a saucer and roll the garlic slices in it to coat. Slide the garlic slices and the cloves into the pockets in the pork. Season the meat all over with salt and pepper.

Place the pork in a large ovenproof dish or roasting tin. Pour in the wine and water. Cook in the preheated oven, basting the meat occasionally, for 2½–2¾ hours, until the pork is tender but still quite moist.

If you are serving the pork hot, transfer it to a carving board and cut into slices. If you are serving it cold, let it cool completely in the cooking juices before removing and slicing.

roman pan-fried lamb

Chunks of tender lamb, pan-fried with garlic and stewed in red wine is a real Roman dish.

INGREDIENTS
1 tbsp oil
1 tbsp butter
600 g/1 lb 5 oz lamb (shoulder or leg),
    cut into 2.5-cm/1-inch chunks
4 garlic cloves, peeled
3 sprigs thyme, stalks removed
6 canned anchovy fillets
150 ml/5 fl oz red wine
150 ml/5 fl oz Vegetable Stock (see page 29)
1 tsp sugar
50 g/1¾ oz black olives, stoned and halved
2 tbsp chopped parsley, to garnish
mashed potato, to serve

Heat the oil and butter in a large frying pan. Add the lamb and cook for 4–5 minutes, stirring, until the meat is browned all over.

Using a pestle and mortar, grind together the garlic, thyme and anchovies to make a smooth paste.

Add the wine and Vegetable Stock to the pan. Stir in the garlic, thyme and anchovy paste together with the sugar.

Bring the mixture to the boil, reduce the heat, cover and simmer for 30–40 minutes or until the lamb is tender. For the last 10 minutes of the cooking time, remove the lid to allow the sauce to reduce slightly.

Stir the olives into the sauce and mix to combine.

Transfer the lamb and the sauce to a serving bowl and garnish. Serve with creamy mashed potatoes.

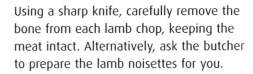

serves 4 | prep 10 mins | cook 35 mins

lamb with bay & lemon

These lamb chops quickly become more elegant when the bone is removed to make noisettes.

INGREDIENTS
4 lamb chops
1 tbsp oil
1 tbsp butter
150 ml/5 fl oz white wine
150 ml/5 fl oz Vegetable Stock (see page 29)
2 bay leaves
pared rind of 1 lemon
salt and pepper

Using a sharp knife, carefully remove the bone from each lamb chop, keeping the meat intact. Alternatively, ask the butcher to prepare the lamb noisettes for you.

Shape the meat into rounds and secure with a length of string.

In a large frying pan, heat together the oil and butter until the mixture starts to froth.

Add the lamb noisettes to the frying pan and cook for 2–3 minutes on each side or until browned all over.

Remove the frying pan from the heat, drain off all of the excess fat and discard.

Return the frying pan to the heat. Add the wine, Vegetable Stock, bay leaves and lemon rind to the frying pan and cook for 20–25 minutes or until the lamb is tender. Season the lamb noisettes and sauce to taste with a little salt and pepper.

Transfer to serving plates. Remove the string from each noisette and serve with the sauce.

serves 4 | prep 15 mins | cook 1 hr 30 mins

lamb with olives

This is a very simple dish, and the chilli adds a bit of spiciness. It is quick to prepare and makes an ideal supper dish.

INGREDIENTS
1.25 kg/2 lb 12 oz boned leg of lamb
90 ml/6 tbsp olive oil
2 garlic cloves, crushed
1 onion, sliced
1 small red chilli, deseeded and
  finely chopped
175 ml/6 fl oz dry white wine
50 g/1¾ stoned black olives
salt
chopped fresh parsley, to garnish
focaccia or crusty white bread, to serve

Preheat the oven to 180°C/350°F/ Gas Mark 4. Using a sharp knife, cut the lamb into small cubes, about 2.5 cm/1 inch.

Heat the oil in a frying pan and fry the garlic, onion and chilli for 5 minutes.

Add the meat and wine and cook for a further 5 minutes.

Stir in the olives, then transfer the mixture to a casserole. Place in the preheated oven and cook for 1 hour 20 minutes, or until the meat is tender. Season to taste with salt, garnish with chopped parsley and serve with focaccia.

serves 4 | prep 25 mins | cook 2 hrs

lamb shanks with roasted onions

Slow-roasted lamb is infused with the flavours of garlic and rosemary and served with sweet red onions and glazed carrot batons. You won't require anything more except a bottle of fruity red wine.

INGREDIENTS
4 x 350 g/12 oz lamb shanks
6 garlic cloves
2 tbsp virgin olive oil
1 tbsp very finely chopped fresh rosemary
4 red onions
350 g/12 oz carrots, cut into thin batons
4 tbsp water
salt and pepper

Preheat the oven to 180°C/350°F/Gas Mark 4. Trim off any excess fat from the lamb. Using a small, sharp knife, make six incisions in each shank. Cut the garlic cloves lengthways into four slices. Insert six garlic slices in the incisions in each lamb shank.

Place the lamb in a single layer in a roasting tin, drizzle with the olive oil, sprinkle with the rosemary and season with pepper. Roast in the preheated oven for 45 minutes.

Wrap each of the onions in a square of foil. Remove the tin from the oven and season the lamb shanks with salt. Return the tin to the oven and place the onions on the shelf next to it. Roast for a further 1–1¼ hours, until the lamb is very tender.

Meanwhile, bring a large saucepan of water to the boil. Add the carrot batons to the boiling water and blanch for 1 minute. Drain and refresh under cold water.

Remove the tin from the oven when the lamb is meltingly tender and transfer the meat to a warmed serving dish. Skim off any fat from the tin and place it over a medium heat. Add the carrots and cook for 2 minutes, then add the water, bring to the boil and simmer, stirring constantly and scraping up the glazed bits from the base of the tin.

Transfer the carrots and sauce to the serving dish. Remove the onions from the oven and unwrap. Cut off and discard about 1 cm/½ inch of the tops and add the onions to the dish. Serve immediately.

serves 4 | prep 35 mins | cook 3 hrs

pot-roasted leg of lamb

This dish from Abruzzo uses a slow cooking method which ensures that the meat becomes very tender.

INGREDIENTS
1.75 kg/3 lb 12 oz leg of lamb
3–4 sprigs fresh rosemary
125 g/4½ oz streaky bacon rashers
4 tbsp olive oil
2–3 garlic cloves, crushed
2 onions, sliced
2 carrots, sliced
2 celery sticks, sliced
300 ml/10 fl oz dry white wine
1 tbsp tomato purée
300 ml/10 fl oz Vegetable Stock
   (see page 29)
350 g/12 oz tomatoes, peeled, cut into
   quarters and deseeded
1 tbsp chopped fresh parsley
1 tbsp chopped fresh oregano or marjoram
salt and pepper
fresh rosemary sprigs, to garnish

Preheat the oven to 180°C/350°F/Gas Mark 4. Wipe the lamb all over, trimming off any excess fat, then season well with salt and pepper, rubbing well in. Lay the sprigs of rosemary over the lamb, cover evenly with the bacon rashers and tie in place with string.

Heat the oil in a frying pan and fry the lamb for about 10 minutes or until brown all over, turning several times. Remove the lamb from the pan.

Transfer the oil from the pan to a large flameproof casserole, add the garlic and onion and fry for 3–4 minutes, until they are beginning to soften. Add the carrots and celery and continue to cook for a few minutes longer.

Lay the lamb on top of the vegetables and press down to partly submerge. Pour the wine over the lamb, add the tomato purée and simmer for 3–4 minutes. Add the stock, tomatoes, herbs and seasoning, return to the boil and cook for a further 3–4 minutes.

Cover the casserole tightly and cook in the preheated oven, for 2–2½ hours, until the lamb is very tender.

Remove the lamb from the casserole and, if preferred, take off the bacon and herbs along with the string. Keep warm. Strain the juices, skimming off any excess fat, and serve in a jug. The vegetables may be put around the joint or in a serving dish. Garnish with rosemary sprigs.

serves 4 | prep 20 mins + 30 mins chilling | cook 10 mins

saltimbocca

Originally from Brescia, but now a Roman speciality, saltimbocca literally means 'jump in the mouth', a reflection of just how highly regarded this dish is.

INGREDIENTS
4 veal escalopes
2 tbsp lemon juice
1 tbsp chopped fresh sage leaves
4 slices prosciutto
55 g/2 oz unsalted butter
3 tbsp dry white wine
salt and pepper

Place the veal escalopes between 2 sheets of clingfilm and pound with the flat end of a meat mallet or the side of a rolling pin until very thin. Transfer the scallops to a plate and sprinkle with the lemon juice. Set aside for 30 minutes, spooning the juice over them occasionally.

Pat the escalopes dry with kitchen paper, season with salt and pepper to taste and rub with half the sage. Place a slice of prosciutto on each escalope and secure with a cocktail stick.

Melt the butter in a large, heavy-based frying pan. Add the remaining sage and cook over a low heat, stirring constantly, for 1 minute. Add the escalopes and cook for 3–4 minutes on each side, until golden brown. Pour in the wine and cook for an additional 2 minutes.

Transfer the escalopes to a warmed serving dish and pour the pan juices over them. Remove and discard the cocktail sticks and serve immediately.

COOK'S' TIP
Serve the escalopes with fresh lemon wedges to enhance the delicate flavour of the veal.

serves 4 | prep 25 mins | cook 1 hr 35 mins

vitello tonnato

This cold classic, which needs to be prepared the day before you serve it, combines two favourite Italian ingredients – veal and tuna. If you can only find a ready-rolled loin, you will need to unroll the meat before marinating it.

INGREDIENTS
750 g/1 lb 10 oz loin of veal, boned
2 carrots, thinly sliced
1 onion, thinly sliced
2 celery sticks, thinly sliced
2 cloves
2 bay leaves
1 litre/1¾ pints dry white wine
140 g/5 oz canned tuna, drained
4 anchovy fillets, drained and finely chopped
55 g/2 oz capers, rinsed and finely chopped
55 g/2 oz gherkins, drained and finely chopped
2 egg yolks
4 tbsp lemon juice
125 ml/4 fl oz extra virgin olive oil
salt and pepper

to garnish
lemon slices
fresh flat-leaved parsley, finely chopped

Place the veal in a large, non-metallic dish and add the carrots, onion, celery, cloves and bay leaves. Pour in the wine and turn the veal to coat. Cover with clingfilm and put in the refrigerator to marinate overnight.

Drain the veal, reserving the marinade, and roll the meat before wrapping it in a piece of muslin, tying it with string so that it holds its shape. Place the veal in a large saucepan. Pour the marinade into another saucepan and bring to the boil. Pour it over the veal and add enough boiling water to cover. Season with salt and pepper, bring back to the boil, then reduce the heat, cover and simmer for 1½ hours, until tender but still firm.

Transfer the veal to a plate and set aside to cool completely, then chill until ready to serve. Strain the cooking liquid into a bowl and set aside to cool.

Combine the tuna, anchovies, capers and gherkins in a bowl or process in a food processor or blender to make a purée. Beat the egg yolks with the lemon juice in another bowl. Gradually beat in the olive oil, adding it drop by drop to start with and then in a steady stream. When all the oil has been incorporated, stir in the tuna mixture and about 2 tablespoons of the cooled cooking liquid to give the consistency of double cream. Season to taste with salt and pepper. Cover with clingfilm and put in the refrigerator until required.

To serve, unwrap the veal and pat it dry with kitchen paper. Using a sharp knife, cut the meat into 3–5-mm/⅛–¼-inch thick slices and arrange them on a serving platter. Stir the tuna sauce and spoon it over the veal. Garnish with lemon slices and parsley and serve.

serves 4 | prep 15 mins | cook 1 hr 20 mins

osso bucco

This rich stew of veal, onions and leeks is Milan's signature dish. It is traditionally served with the saffron-flavoured risotto known as risotto alla Milanese.

INGREDIENTS
1 tbsp virgin olive oil
4 tbsp butter
2 onions, chopped
1 leek, chopped
3 tbsp plain flour
4 thick slices of veal shin (osso bucco)
300 ml/10 fl oz white wine
300 ml/10 fl oz Chicken Stock (see page 29)
salt and pepper

gremolata
2 tbsp chopped fresh parsley
1 garlic clove, finely chopped
grated rind of 1 lemon

Heat the oil and butter in a large, heavy-based frying pan. Add the onions and leek and cook over a low heat, stirring occasionally, for 5 minutes, until softened.

Spread out the flour on a plate and season with salt and pepper. Toss the pieces of veal in the flour to coat, shaking off any excess. Add the veal to the frying pan, increase the heat to high and cook until browned on both sides.

Gradually stir in the wine and stock and bring just to the boil, stirring constantly. Reduce the heat, cover and simmer for 1¼ hours, or until the veal is very tender.

Meanwhile, make the gremolata by mixing the parsley, garlic and lemon rind together in a small bowl.

Transfer the veal to a warmed serving dish with a slotted spoon. Bring the sauce to the boil and cook, stirring occasionally, until thickened and reduced. Pour the sauce over the veal, sprinkle with the gremolata and serve immediately.

VARIATION
Modern versions of this dish often include tomatoes. If you like, add 400 g/14 oz canned tomatoes with the wine and stock. You could also add 1 finely chopped carrot and 1 finely chopped celery stick with the onions and leek.

serves 4 | prep 15 mins | cook 35 mins

sausage & bean casserole

In this traditional Tuscan dish, Italian sausages are cooked with cannellini beans and tomatoes.

INGREDIENTS
1 green pepper
8 Italian sausages
1 tbsp olive oil
1 large onion, chopped
2 garlic cloves, chopped
225g/8 oz fresh tomatoes, peeled (see Cook's Tip, page 111) and chopped or 400 g/14 oz canned tomatoes, chopped
2 tbsp sun-dried tomato purée
400 g/14 oz canned cannellini beans
mashed potato or rice, to serve

Using a sharp knife, deseed the green pepper and cut it into thin strips.

Prick the Italian sausages all over with a fork. Cook the sausages under a preheated grill for 10–12 minutes, turning occasionally, until brown all over. Set the sausages aside and keep warm.

Heat the oil in a large frying pan. Add the onion, garlic and green pepper to the frying pan and cook for 5 minutes, stirring occasionally, or until softened.

Add the tomatoes to the frying pan and leave the mixture to simmer for about 5 minutes, stirring occasionally, or until slightly reduced and thickened.

Stir the sun-dried tomato purée, cannellini beans and Italian sausages into the mixture in the frying pan. Cook for 4–5 minutes or until the mixture is piping hot. If the mixture becomes too dry during cooking, add 4–5 tablespoons of water.

Transfer the casserole to serving plates and serve with mashed potato or cooked rice.

serves 4 | prep 15 mins | cook 1 hr 20 mins

tuscan chicken

Another robust casserole, which is good served with plenty of fresh crusty bread or ribbon pasta, such as tagliatelle, fettuccine or tagliarini.

INGREDIENTS
2 tbsp plain flour
4 skinless chicken portions
3 tbsp olive oil
1 red onion, chopped
2 garlic cloves, chopped finely
1 red pepper, deseeded and chopped
pinch of saffron threads
150 ml/5 fl oz Chicken Stock
   (see page 29)
400 g/14 oz canned tomatoes, chopped
4 sun-dried tomatoes in oil, drained and
   chopped
225 g/8 oz field mushrooms, sliced
115 g/4 oz black olives, stoned
4 tbsp lemon juice
salt and pepper
fresh basil leaves, to garnish

Preheat the oven to 180°C/350°F/ Gas Mark 4. Place the flour on a shallow plate and season with salt and pepper. Coat the chicken in the seasoned flour, shaking off any excess. Heat the olive oil in a large flameproof casserole. Add the chicken and cook over a medium heat, turning frequently, for 5–7 minutes, until golden brown in colour. Remove from the casserole and set aside.

Add the onion, garlic and red pepper to the casserole, reduce the heat and cook, stirring occasionally, for 5 minutes or until soft. Meanwhile, stir the saffron into the stock.

Stir the tomatoes with their can juices, the sun-dried tomatoes, mushrooms and olives into the casserole and cook, stirring occasionally, for 3 minutes. Pour in the stock and saffron mixture and the lemon juice. Bring to the boil, then return the chicken to the casserole.

Cover and cook in the preheated oven for 1 hour, until the chicken is tender and the juices run clear when a skewer is inserted into the thickest part of the meat. Garnish with basil and serve immediately.

serves 4 | prep 10 mins | cook 1 hr 15 mins

chicken cacciatora

The sun-dried tomato flavour adds a welcome reminder of summer to this hearty warming winter recipe.

INGREDIENTS
15 g/½ oz unsalted butter
2 tbsp olive oil
1.8 kg/4 lb skinless chicken portions, bone in
2 red onions, sliced
2 garlic cloves, chopped finely
400 g/14 oz canned tomatoes, chopped
2 tbsp chopped fresh flat-leaved parsley
6 fresh basil leaves, torn
1 tbsp sun-dried tomato purée
150 ml/5 fl oz red wine
salt and pepper
225 g/8 oz field mushrooms, sliced

Preheat the oven to 160°C/325°F/ Gas Mark 3. Melt the butter with the olive oil in a flameproof casserole. Add the chicken and cook, turning frequently, for 5–10 minutes, until golden brown all over. Transfer the chicken to a plate, using a slotted spoon, and set aside.

Add the onions and garlic to the casserole and cook over a low heat, stirring occasionally, for 10 minutes, until golden. Add the tomatoes with their can juices, the parsley, basil, tomato purée and wine, and season to taste with salt and pepper. Bring to the boil, then return the chicken pieces to the casserole, pushing them down into the sauce.

Cover and cook in the preheated oven for 50 minutes. Add the mushrooms and cook for a further 10 minutes, until the chicken is tender and the juices run clear when a skewer is inserted into the thickest part of the meat. Serve immediately.

serves 4 | prep 30 mins | cook 45 mins

prosciutto-wrapped chicken

*Stuffed with ricotta, nutmeg and spinach,
the chicken breasts are then wrapped in
wafer-thin slices of prosciutto di Parma
and gently cooked in white wine.*

INGREDIENTS
125 g/4½ oz frozen spinach, defrosted
125 g/4½ oz ricotta cheese
pinch of grated nutmeg
4 skinless, boneless chicken breasts,
   weighing 175 g/6 oz each
4 prosciutto di Parma slices
2 tbsp butter
1 tbsp olive oil
12 small onions or shallots
125 g/4½ oz button
   mushrooms, sliced
1 tbsp plain flour
150 ml/5 fl oz dry white or red wine
300 ml/10 fl oz Chicken Stock
   (see page 29)
salt and pepper
carrot purée and French beans, to serve

Preheat the oven to 200°C/400°F/Gas Mark 6. Put the spinach into
a sieve and press out the water with a spoon. Mix with the ricotta
cheese and nutmeg and season to taste with salt and pepper.

Using a sharp knife, slit each chicken breast through the side and
enlarge each cut to form a pocket. Fill with the spinach mixture,
reshape the chicken breasts, wrap each breast tightly in a slice of
prosciutto and secure with a cocktail stick. Cover the chicken and
chill in the refrigerator.

Heat the butter and oil in a frying pan and brown the chicken
breasts for 2 minutes on each side. Transfer the chicken to a large,
shallow ovenproof dish and keep warm until required.

Fry the onions and mushrooms for 2–3 minutes until lightly
browned. Stir in the flour, then gradually add the wine and stock.
Bring to the boil, stirring constantly. Season with salt and pepper
and spoon the mixture around the chicken.

Cook the chicken, uncovered, in the preheated oven for 20 minutes.
Turn and cook for a further 10 minutes, until the chicken is tender
and the juices run clear when a skewer is inserted into the thickest
part of the meat. Remove the cocktail sticks and serve on warmed
plates with the sauce, together with carrot purée and French beans.

serves 6 | prep 35 mins | cook 2 hrs

italian-style sunday roast

A mixture of cheese, rosemary, and sun-dried tomatoes is stuffed under the skin of the chicken, which is then roasted with garlic, potatoes and vegetables.

INGREDIENTS
chicken, weighing 2.5 kg/5 lb 8 oz
sprigs of fresh rosemary
175 g/6 oz feta cheese, coarsely grated
2 tbsp sun-dried tomato purée
4 tbsp butter, softened
1 bulb garlic
1 kg/2 lb 4 oz new potatoes, halved if large
1 each red, green and yellow pepper,
  cut into chunks
3 courgettes, thinly sliced
2 tbsp olive oil
2 tbsp plain flour
600 ml/1 pint Chicken Stock (see page 29)
salt and pepper

Preheat the oven to 190°C/375°F/ Gas Mark 5. Rinse the chicken inside and out with cold water and drain well. Carefully cut between the skin and the top of the breast meat using a small pointed knife. Slide a finger into the slit and carefully enlarge it to form a pocket. Continue until the skin is completely lifted away from both breasts and the top of the legs.

Chop the leaves from 3 rosemary stems. Mix with the feta cheese, sun-dried tomato purée, butter and pepper to taste, then spoon under the skin. Put the chicken in a large roasting tin, cover with foil and cook in the preheated oven for 20 minutes per 500 g/1 lb 2 oz, plus 20 minutes, until the chicken is tender and the juices run clear when a skewer is inserted into the thickest part of the meat.

Break the garlic bulb into cloves but do not peel. Add the vegetables to the chicken after 40 minutes. Drizzle with oil, tuck in a few stems of rosemary and season with salt and pepper. Cook for the remaining calculated time, removing the foil for the last 40 minutes to brown the chicken.

Transfer the chicken to a serving platter. Place some of the vegetables around the chicken and transfer the remainder to a warmed serving dish. Pour the fat out of the roasting tin and stir the flour into the remaining tin juices. Cook for 2 minutes then gradually stir in the stock. Bring to the boil, stirring until thickened. Strain into a sauce boat and serve with the chicken.

serves 4 | prep 15 mins | cook 1 hr 30 mins

chicken with green olives

Olives are a popular flavouring for poultry and game in the Apulia region, where this recipe originates.

INGREDIENTS
3 tbsp olive oil
2 tbsp butter
4 chicken breasts, part boned
1 large onion, chopped finely
2 garlic cloves, crushed
2 red, yellow or green peppers,
    deseeded and cut into large pieces
250 g/9 oz button mushrooms, sliced
    or cut into quarters
175 g/6 oz tomatoes, peeled (see Cook's tip,
    page 111) and halved
150 ml/5 fl oz dry white wine
175 g/6 oz stoned green olives
4-6 tbsp double cream
400 g/14 oz dried pasta
salt and pepper
chopped fresh flat-leaved parsley, to garnish

Preheat the oven to 180°C/350°F/
Gas Mark 4. Heat 2 tablespoons of the oil and the butter in a frying pan. Add the chicken breasts and fry until golden brown all over. Remove the chicken from the pan.

Add the onion and garlic to the pan and fry over a medium heat until beginning to soften. Add the peppers and mushrooms and cook for 2–3 minutes. Add the tomatoes and season to taste with salt and pepper. Transfer the vegetables to a casserole and arrange the chicken on top.

Add the wine to the pan, bring to the boil and Pour over the chicken. Cover and cook in the preheated oven for 50 minutes, or

until the chicken is tender and the juices run clear when a skewer is inserted into the thickest part of the meat.

Add the olives to the casserole and mix in. Pour in the cream, cover and return to the oven for 10–20 minutes.

Meanwhile, bring a large, heavy-based saucepan of lightly salted water to the boil. Add the pasta and the remaining oil and cook for 8–10 minutes, or until the pasta is tender but still 'al dente'. Drain well and transfer to a warmed serving dish.

Arrange the chicken on top of the pasta, spoon over the sauce, garnish with the parsley and serve immediately. Alternatively, place the pasta in a large serving bowl and serve separately.

serves 4 | prep 15 mins | cook 40 mins

chicken peperonata

All the sunshine colours and flavours of Italy are combined in this easy dish.

INGREDIENTS
8 chicken thighs
2 tbsp wholemeal flour
2 tbsp olive oil
1 small onion, thinly sliced
1 garlic clove, crushed
1 each large red, yellow and green
 peppers, deseeded and thinly sliced
400 g/14 oz canned chopped tomatoes
1 tbsp chopped oregano
salt and pepper
fresh oregano, to garnish

Remove the skin from the chicken thighs and toss them in the flour.

Heat the oil in a wide frying pan add the chicken and fry over a high heat until sealed and lightly browned, then remove from the pan.

Add the onion to the pan and fry until soft. Add the garlic, peppers, tomatoes and oregano, then bring to the boil, stirring.

Arrange the chicken over the vegetables, season to taste with salt and pepper, then cover the pan tightly and simmer for 20–25 minutes, or until the chicken is tender and the juices run clear when a skewer is inserted into the thickest part of the meat.

Garnish with oregano and serve immediately.

COOK'S TIP
For extra flavour, halve the peppers and grill under a preheated grill until the skins are charred. Leave to cool, then remove the skins and seeds. Slice the peppers thinly and use them in the recipe.

serves 4 | prep 25 mins | cook 20 mins

chicken with smoked ham & parmesan

There is much more to the cuisine of Bologna than the eponymous pasta dish, as it is renowned for its rich dishes. The capital of the Emilia-Romagna region, Bologna is nicknamed La Grassa – the fat, rich and plentiful one.

INGREDIENTS
4 skinned, boned chicken breasts
2 tbsp plain flour
55 g/2 oz unsalted butter
8 thin slices smoked ham, trimmed
55 g/2 oz freshly grated Parmesan cheese
fresh basil sprigs, to garnish
salt and pepper

Cut each chicken breast through the thickest part to open them out, then place the pieces between two sheets of clingfilm and pound with the flat end of a meat mallet or the side of a rolling pin until they are as thin as possible. Spread out the flour on a shallow plate and season with salt and pepper. Coat the chicken pieces in the seasoned flour, shaking off any excess.

Melt half the butter in a large, heavy-based frying pan. Add the chicken pieces, in batches if necessary, and cook over a medium heat, turning frequently, for 10–15 minutes, until they are golden brown, cooked through and the juices run clear when a skewer is inserted into the thickest part of the meat.

Meanwhile, melt the remaining butter in a

small saucepan. Remove the chicken from the heat. Place a slice of ham on each piece of chicken, sprinkle with cheese, pour the butter over and return to the heat for 3–4 minutes, until the cheese has melted. Serve immediately, garnished with basil.

VARIATION
A similar dish is made in the Valle d'Aosta, but instead of the chicken breasts being cut and opened out, they are slit to make a pocket. The pockets are then filled with slices of smoked ham or prosciutto and Fontina cheese before cooking.

serves 4 | prep 10 mins | cook 35 mins

chicken & balsamic vinegar

A rich caramelized sauce, flavoured with balsamic vinegar and wine, adds a piquant flavour. The chicken needs to be marinated overnight.

INGREDIENTS
4 boneless chicken thighs
2 garlic cloves, crushed
175 ml/6 fl oz red wine
3 tbsp white wine vinegar
1 tbsp oil
1 tbsp butter
6 shallots
3 tbsp balsamic vinegar
2 tbsp fresh thyme
salt and pepper
cooked polenta or rice, to serve

Using a sharp knife, make a few slashes in the chicken skin. Brush the chicken with the crushed garlic and place in a non-metallic dish.

Pour the wine and white wine vinegar over the chicken and season to taste with salt and pepper. Cover and leave to marinate in the refrigerator overnight.

Remove the chicken pieces with a slotted spoon, draining well, and reserve the marinade.

Heat the oil and butter in a frying pan. Add the shallots and cook for 2–3 minutes or until they begin to soften.

Add the chicken pieces to the pan and cook for 3–4 minutes, turning, until brown all over. Reduce the heat and add half of the reserved marinade. Cover and cook for 15–20 minutes, adding more marinade when necessary.

Cook until the chicken is tender and the juices run clear when a skewer is inserted into the thickest part of the meat. Add the balsamic vinegar and thyme and cook for a further 4 minutes.

Transfer the chicken and marinade to warmed serving plates and serve with polenta.

serves 4 | prep 30 mins | cook 3 hrs 30 mins

lombardy duck

Rich meat, such as duck and goose, is combined with lentils in the cuisines of many countries and Italy is no exception. This is a wonderfully flavoursome dish that would be a good choice when entertaining as it can be prepared in advance and gently reheated.

INGREDIENTS
2.25 kg/5 lb duck
225 g/8 oz small brown lentils, rinsed
1 tbsp virgin olive oil, plus extra for frying
2 onions
2 celery sticks
2 tbsp brandy or grappa
150 ml/5 fl oz dry white wine
1 tsp cornflour
salt and pepper

stock
1 celery stick
1 garlic clove
6 peppercorns, crushed lightly
1 bay leaf
5 sprigs fresh flat-leaved parsley
1 onion
1 clove
salt

Cut the duck into joints. Cut off the wings. Fold back the skin at the neck end and cut out the wishbone with a small, sharp knife. Using poultry shears or heavy kitchen scissors, cut the duck breast in half along the breastbone, from the tail end to the neck. Cut along each side of the backbone to separate the two halves. Remove the backbone. Cut each portion in half diagonally.

To make the stock, place the wings and backbone in a large saucepan and add the celery, garlic, peppercorns, bay leaf and parsley. Stick the onion with the clove and add to the pan with a large pinch of salt. Add cold water to cover and bring to the boil. Skim off any scum that rises to the surface. Reduce the heat and simmer very gently for 2 hours. Strain into a clean saucepan and boil until reduced. Measure 150 ml/5 fl oz and set aside.

Place the lentils in a saucepan with enough cold water to cover. Add the olive oil. Cut 1 onion in half and add to the pan with 1 celery stick. Bring to the boil over a medium heat, reduce the heat and simmer for 15 minutes, until the lentils are starting to soften. Drain and set aside.

Meanwhile, put the duck portions, skin-side down, in a heavy-based frying pan and cook, shaking the pan occasionally, for 10 minutes. Transfer the duck portions to a flameproof casserole and drain off the excess fat from the pan. Finely chop the remaining onion and celery and add to the pan. Cook over a low heat, stirring occasionally, for 5 minutes, until soft. Using a slotted spoon, transfer the vegetables to the casserole.

Set the casserole over a medium heat, add the brandy and ignite. When the flames have died down, add the wine and the reserved measured stock. Bring to the boil, add the lentils and season with salt and pepper. Cover and simmer over a low heat for 40 minutes.

Combine the cornflour with 2 tablespoons of the stock to make a smooth paste in a small bowl. Stir the paste into the casserole and cook, stirring frequently, for about 5 minutes, until thickened. Taste and adjust the seasoning, if necessary, and serve immediately.

serves 4 | prep 15 mins | cook 40 mins

pesto-baked partridge

*Partridge has a more delicate flavour
than many game birds and this subtle
sauce perfectly complements it.*

INGREDIENTS
8 partridge pieces, about 115 g/4 oz each
4 tbsp butter, melted
4 tbsp Dijon mustard
2 tbsp lime juice
1 tbsp brown sugar
6 tbsp Green Pesto Sauce (see page 28)
450 g/1 lb dried rigatoni
1 tbsp olive oil
115 g/4 oz freshly grated Parmesan cheese
salt and pepper

Preheat the oven to 200°C/400°F/Gas Mark 6. Arrange the partridge
pieces, smooth side down, in a single layer in a large, ovenproof dish.

Mix together the butter, mustard, lime juice and sugar in a bowl.
Season to taste with salt and pepper. Brush this mixture over the
partridge pieces and bake in the preheated oven for 15 minutes.

Remove the dish from the oven and coat the partridge pieces with
3 tablespoons of the Green Pesto Sauce. Return to the oven and
bake for a further 12 minutes.

Remove the dish from the oven and carefully turn over the partridge
pieces. Coat the top of the partridge pieces with the remaining
mustard mixture and return to the oven for a further 10 minutes.

Meanwhile, bring a large, heavy-based saucepan of lightly
salted water to the boil. Add the rigatoni and oil and cook for
8–10 minutes, until the pasta is tender, but still 'al dente'. Drain
and transfer to a warmed serving dish and toss with the remaining
Green Pesto Sauce and the Parmesan cheese.

Serve the partridge with the pasta, pouring over the cooking juices.

VARIATION
*You could also prepare young pheasant
in the same way.*

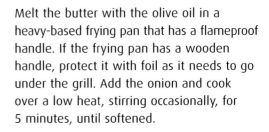

serves 3 | prep 10 mins | cook 30 mins

seafood omelette

This substantial omelette makes a quick and easy mid-week supper dish – a nourishing main course for a family meal. For a larger family, double the quantity and use two frying pans.

INGREDIENTS
2 tbsp unsalted butter
1 tbsp olive oil
1 onion, very finely chopped
175 g/6 oz courgettes, halved lengthways
  and sliced
1 celery stick, very finely chopped
85 g/3 oz button mushrooms, sliced
55 g/2 oz French beans, cut into
  5-cm/2-inch lengths
4 eggs
85 g/3½ oz mascarpone cheese
1 tbsp chopped fresh thyme
1 tbsp shredded fresh basil
200 g/7 oz canned tuna, drained and flaked
115 g/4 oz peeled cooked prawns
salt and pepper

Melt the butter with the olive oil in a heavy-based frying pan that has a flameproof handle. If the frying pan has a wooden handle, protect it with foil as it needs to go under the grill. Add the onion and cook over a low heat, stirring occasionally, for 5 minutes, until softened.

Add the courgettes, celery, mushrooms and beans and cook, stirring occasionally, for an additional 8–10 minutes, until the mixture is starting to brown.

Beat the eggs with the mascarpone, thyme, basil and salt and pepper to taste.

Add the tuna to the frying pan and stir it into the mixture with a wooden spoon. Add the prawns last.

Pour the egg mixture into the frying pan and cook for 5 minutes, until it is just starting to set. Draw the egg from the sides of the frying pan towards the centre to let the uncooked egg run underneath.

Put the frying pan under a preheated grill and cook until the egg is just set and the surface is starting to brown. Cut the omelette into wedges and serve.

serves 4 | prep 20 mins + 30 mins resting | cook 30 mins

deep-fried seafood

Like many seafood recipes, this popular dish comes from the Campania region of southern Italy. It invariably contains a mixture of white fish fillets and shellfish, but the precise ingredients will depend on the day's catch.

INGREDIENTS
corn oil, for frying
200 g/7 oz white fish fillets, such as lemon sole, skinned and cut into strips
200 g/7 oz monkfish fillets, cut into bite-sized chunks
4 shelled scallops, with or without corals
225 g/8 oz large cooked prawns, peeled but with the tails intact
fresh flat-leaf parsley sprigs and lemon wedges, to garnish
salt

batter
115 g/4 oz plain flour
1 egg yolk
1 tbsp olive oil
225 ml/8 fl oz milk
2 egg whites

First, make the batter. Sift the flour with a pinch of salt into a bowl and make a well in the centre. Add the egg yolk and olive oil to the well and mix together with a wooden spoon, gradually incorporating the flour. Gradually beat in the milk to make a smooth batter. Cover and set aside to rest for 30 minutes.

Heat the corn oil in a deep-fryer to 180–190°C/350–375°F or, if using a heavy-based frying pan, until a cube of day-old bread browns in 30 seconds.

Meanwhile, whisk the egg whites in another bowl until they form stiff peaks, then gently fold them into the batter.

Using tongs, dip the fish and shellfish, a piece at a time, into the batter to coat, then add to the frying pan and cook for 3–4 minutes, until crisp and golden. Do not overcrowd the frying pan. As each piece is cooked, remove it from the frying pan and drain on kitchen paper. Transfer to a serving platter and keep warm while you cook the remaining fish and shellfish. Garnish with parsley and lemon wedges and serve.

serves 4 | prep 25 mins | cook 30 mins

roast sea bream with fennel

All sea bream – and it is quite a large family of fish – is delicately flavoured and especially delicious when stuffed and roasted. If possible, try to obtain gilt head sea bream, known as orata in Italy, for this recipe.

INGREDIENTS
250 g/9 oz dried, uncoloured breadcrumbs
2 tbsp milk
1 fennel bulb, sliced thinly, fronds reserved
  for garnish
1 tbsp lemon juice
2 tbsp Sambuca*
1 tbsp chopped fresh thyme
1 bay leaf, crumbled
1.5 kg/3 lb 5 oz whole sea bream, cleaned,
  scaled and boned
3 tbsp olive oil, plus extra for brushing
1 red onion, chopped
300 ml/10 fl oz dry white wine
salt and pepper

Preheat the oven to 240°C/475°F/ Gas Mark 9. Place the breadcrumbs in a bowl, add the milk and set aside for 5 minutes to soak. Place the fennel in another bowl and add the lemon juice, Sambuca, thyme and bay leaf. Squeeze the breadcrumbs and add them to the mixture, stirring well.

Rinse the fish inside and out under cold running water and pat dry with paper towels. Season with salt and pepper. Spoon the fennel mixture into the cavity, then bind the fish with trussing thread or kitchen string.

Brush a large ovenproof dish with olive oil and sprinkle the onion over the base. Lay the fish on top and pour in the wine – it should reach about one third of the way up the fish. Drizzle the fish with the oil and cook in the preheated oven for 25–30 minutes. Baste the fish occasionally with the cooking juices and, if it starts to brown, cover it with foil to protect it.

Carefully lift out the fish, remove the string and place on a warmed serving platter. Garnish with the reserved fennel fronds and serve immediately.

COOK'S TIP
Sambuca is an Italian liqueur distilled from witch elder, but it has a strong aniseed flavour, which marries well with fish. If it is unavailable, substitute Pernod.

serves 4 | prep 15 mins | cook 35 mins

swordfish with olives & capers

Swordfish is plentiful in the waters surrounding Sicily, where it is usually cooked with traditional Mediterranean ingredients. This recipe comes from Palermo, Sicily's main port.

INGREDIENTS
2 tbsp plain flour
4 x 225 g/8 oz swordfish steaks
100 ml/3½ fl oz olive oil
2 garlic cloves, halved
1 onion, chopped
4 anchovy fillets, drained and chopped
4 tomatoes, peeled (see Cook's Tip, page 111), seeded and chopped
12 green olives, stoned and sliced
1 tbsp capers, rinsed
salt and pepper
fresh rosemary leaves, to garnish

Spread out the flour on a plate and season with salt and pepper. Coat the fish in the seasoned flour, shaking off any excess.

Gently heat the olive oil in a large, heavy-based frying pan. Add the garlic and cook over a low heat for 2–3 minutes, until just golden. Do not let it turn brown or burn. Remove the garlic and discard.

Add the fish to the frying pan and cook over a medium heat for about 4 minutes on each side, until cooked through and golden brown. Remove the steaks from the frying pan and set aside.

Add the onion and anchovies to the frying pan and cook, mashing the anchovies with a wooden spoon until they have turned to a purée and the onion is golden. Add the tomatoes and cook over a low heat, stirring occasionally, for about 20 minutes, until the mixture has thickened.

Stir in the olives and capers and taste and adjust the seasoning. Return the steaks to the frying pan and heat through gently. Serve garnished with rosemary.

serves 8 | prep 1 hr 15 mins | cook 1 hr 30 mins

sole fillets in marsala

A rich wine and cream sauce makes this an excellent dinner party dish. Make the stock the day before to cut down on the preparation time.

INGREDIENTS
1 tbsp peppercorns, crushed lightly
8 sole fillets
90 ml/3 fl oz Marsala
150 ml/5 fl oz double cream
freshly cooked vegetables, to serve

stock
600 ml/1 pint water
bones and skin from the sole fillets
1 onion, peeled and halved
1 carrot, peeled and halved
3 fresh bay leaves

sauce
1 tbsp olive oil
1 tbsp butter
4 shallots, finely chopped
100 g/3½ oz baby button mushrooms, wiped and halved

To make the stock, place the water, fish bones and skin, onion, carrot and bay leaves in a large saucepan and bring to the boil.

Reduce the heat and leave the mixture to simmer for 1 hour or until the stock has reduced to about 150 ml/5 fl oz. Drain the stock through a fine sieve, discarding the bones and vegetables, and set aside.

To make the sauce, heat the oil and butter in a frying pan. Add the shallots and cook, stirring, for 2–3 minutes or until softened.

Add the mushrooms to the frying pan and cook, stirring, for a further 2–3 minutes or until they are just beginning to brown.

Add the peppercorns and sole fillets to the frying pan in batches. Fry the sole fillets for 3–4 minutes on each side or until golden brown. Remove the fish with a slotted spoon, then set aside and keep warm while you cook the remainder.

When all the fillets have been cooked and removed from the frying pan, pour the wine and stock into the frying pan and simmer for 3 minutes. Increase the heat and boil the mixture in the frying pan for about 5 minutes or until the sauce has reduced and thickened.

Pour in the cream and heat through. Pour the sauce over the fish and serve with the cooked vegetables of your choice.

serves 4 | prep 15 mins | cook 40 mins

italian cod

A delicious spiced crunchy topping infuses the fish with flavour and prevents it from losing moisture during cooking.

INGREDIENTS
2 tbsp butter
175 g/6 oz fresh wholemeal breadcrumbs
15 g/½ oz chopped walnuts
grated rind and juice of 2 lemons
2 fresh rosemary sprigs, stalks removed
2 tbsp chopped fresh parsley
4 cod fillets, about
    150 g/5½ oz each
1 garlic clove, crushed
1 small fresh red chilli, diced
3 tbsp walnut oil

Preheat the oven to 200°C/400°F/Gas Mark 6. Melt the butter in a large saucepan over a low heat, stirring constantly. Remove the saucepan from the heat and add the breadcrumbs, walnuts, the rind and juice of 1 lemon, half the rosemary and half the parsley, stirring until mixed.

Press the breadcrumb mixture over the top of the cod fillets. Place the cod fillets in a shallow foil-lined roasting tin. Roast the fish in the oven for 25–30 minutes.

Mix the garlic, the remaining lemon rind and juice, rosemary, parsley and chilli together in a bowl. Beat in the oil and mix to combine. Drizzle the dressing over the cod steaks as soon as they are cooked. Transfer the fish to warmed serving plates and serve immediately.

VARIATION
If preferred, the walnuts may be omitted from the crust. In addition, extra virgin olive oil can be used instead of walnut oil, if you like.

serves 4 | prep 15 mins + 30 mins marinating | cook 15 mins

sicilian tuna

This quick, spicy dish can be cooked in the kitchen or on the barbecue. It needs nothing more than a crisp green salad as an accompaniment.

INGREDIENTS
4 x 140 g/5 oz tuna steaks
2 fennel bulbs, thickly sliced lengthways
2 red onions, sliced
2 tbsp virgin olive oil

marinade
125 ml/4 fl oz extra virgin olive oil
4 garlic cloves, finely chopped
4 fresh red chillies, seeded and
  finely chopped
juice and finely grated rind of 2 lemons
4 tbsp finely chopped fresh flat-leaf parsley
salt and pepper

Make the marinade by whisking all the ingredients together in a bowl. Place the tuna steaks in a large shallow dish and spoon over 4 tablespoons of the marinade, turning to coat. Cover and set aside for 30 minutes. Set aside the remaining marinade.

Heat a ridged griddle pan. Put the fennel and onions in a bowl, add the oil and toss well to coat. Add to the pan and cook for 5 minutes on each side, until just starting to colour. Transfer to serving plates, drizzle with the reserved marinade and keep warm.

Add the tuna to the pan and cook, turning once, for 4–5 minutes, until firm to the touch, but still moist inside. Place the tuna on top of the fennel and onions and serve immediately.

serves 4 | prep 20 mins | cook 45 mins

stuffed squid

*Squid can be tricky to cook properly.
To avoid making it tough, it should either
be cooked very quickly or stewed slowly
on a very low heat in the Italian way.*

INGREDIENTS
8 sun-dried tomatoes
8 small prepared squid, bodies about
    13 cm/5 inches long
85 g/3 oz fresh white breadcrumbs
2 tbsp capers, rinsed and chopped finely
2 tbsp chopped fresh flat-leaved parsley
1 egg white
olive oil, for brushing and drizzling
3 tbsp dry white wine
lemon juice, for drizzling (optional)
salt and pepper

Preheat the oven to 160°C/325°F/
Gas Mark 3. Put the sun-dried tomatoes
in a bowl and cover with boiling water.
Set aside for 15–20 minutes.

Meanwhile, finely chop the squid tentacles
and place in a bowl. Add the breadcrumbs,
capers and parsley.

Thoroughly drain the tomatoes and pat dry
with kitchen paper. Chop them finely and
add to the breadcrumb mixture. Mix
together thoroughly and season to taste
with salt and pepper. Stir in the egg white.

Spoon the breadcrumb mixture into the
squid body sacs, pushing it down well.
Do not fill them more than about three
quarters full or they will burst during
cooking. Secure the opening of each sac
with a cocktail stick.

Generously brush oil over an ovenproof
dish large enough to hold the squid snugly
in a single layer. Place the squid in the dish
and pour in the wine. Cover with foil and
bake in the preheated oven for about
45 minutes, turning and basting occasionally.
Test with a fork to check if the squid is tender.

Remove from the oven and set aside to
cool to room temperature. To serve, remove
and discard the cocktail sticks and slice the
squid into circles. Place on warmed plates
and drizzle with a little olive oil and the
cooled cooking juices or lemon juice, if
using.

serves 4 | prep 15 mins | cook 20 mins

vegetable frittata

*A frittata is a type of Italian omelette –
you can add almost anything to the eggs.
It is also delicious eaten cold and makes
an ideal picnic dish.*

INGREDIENTS
3 tbsp olive oil
1 onion, chopped
2 garlic cloves, chopped
225 g/8 oz courgettes,
   sliced thinly
4 eggs
400 g/14 oz canned borlotti beans,
   drained and rinsed
3 tomatoes, skinned and chopped
2 tbsp chopped fresh parsley
1 tbsp chopped fresh basil
60 g/2¼ oz grated Gruyère cheese
salt and pepper

Heat 2 tablespoons of the oil in a frying pan
with a flameproof handle, add the onion
and garlic and fry gently, stirring occasionally, for 2–3 minutes or until soft. Add the
courgettes and cook for 3–4 minutes, or
until softened.

Break the eggs into a bowl and add salt
and pepper to taste, the fried vegetables,
beans, tomatoes and herbs.

Heat the remaining oil in a 24-cm/9½-inch
omelette pan, add the egg mixture and fry
gently for 5 minutes until the eggs have
almost set and the underside is brown.

Sprinkle the cheese over the top and
place the pan under a preheated moderate
grill for 3–4 minutes or until set
on the top but still moist in the middle.
Cut into wedges and serve warm or at
room temperature.

serves 4 | prep 25 mins | cook 50 mins

spinach & ricotta pie

Preheat the oven to 220°C/425°F/
Gas Mark 7. Rinse the spinach, place in a
large saucepan and cook for 4–5 minutes
until it has wilted. Drain thoroughly. When
the spinach is cool enough to handle,
squeeze out the excess liquid.

Preheat the grill to medium. Place the pine
kernels on a baking tray and lightly toast
under the preheated grill for 2–3 minutes,
or until golden.

Place the ricotta cheese, spinach and eggs
(reserving a small amount for brushing the
pastry top) in a bowl and mix together. Add
the pine kernels, beat well, then stir in the
ground almonds and Parmesan cheese.

Roll out the puff pastry and make two
20-cm/8-inch squares. Trim the edges,
reserving the pastry trimmings. Place
1 pastry square on a baking tray. Spoon
over the spinach mixture, keeping within
1 cm/½ inch of the edge of the pastry.
Brush the edges with beaten egg and
place the second square over the top.

Using a round-bladed knife, press the pastry
edges together by tapping along the sealed
edge. Use the pastry trimmings to make a
few leaves to decorate the pie.

Prick the top of the pie several times with
a fork, brush with beaten egg and bake in
the preheated oven for 10 minutes. Reduce
the oven temperature to 190°C/375°F/
Gas Mark 5 and bake the pie for a further
25–30 minutes.

Although this pie looks very impressive it is actually fairly easy to make. It can be served either hot or cold.

INGREDIENTS
225 g/8 oz spinach
25 g/1 oz pine kernels
100 g/3½ oz ricotta cheese
2 large eggs, beaten
50 g/1¾ oz ground almonds
40 g/1½ oz Parmesan cheese, grated
250 g/9 oz puff pastry, defrosted if frozen
1 small egg, beaten

serves 8 | prep 30 mins | cook 30 mins

roasted pepper terrine

This delicious terrine is an ideal lunch dish. It goes particularly well with Italian bread and a green salad.

INGREDIENTS
3 cups broad beans
6 red peppers, halved and deseeded
3 small courgettes, sliced
   lengthways
1 aubergine, sliced lengthways
3 leeks, halved lengthways
90 ml/6 tbsp olive oil, plus extra for greasing
90 ml/6 tbsp single cream
2 tbsp chopped fresh basil
salt and pepper
fresh basil leaves, to garnish

Preheat the grill to hot. Grease a 1.2-litre/ 2-pint terrine. Blanch the broad beans in boiling water for 1–2 minutes and pop them out of their skins.

Roast the red peppers under the preheated grill for 10–15 minutes, until the skin is black. Remove and put into a polythene bag. Seal and set aside.

Brush the courgettes, aubergine and leeks with 5 tablespoons of the olive oil, and season to taste with salt and pepper. Cook under the hot grill for about 8–10 minutes, until tender, turning once.

Meanwhile, purée the broad beans in a blender or food processor with 1 tablespoon of the olive oil, the cream and the seasoning. Alternatively, chop and then press through a sieve.

Remove the red peppers from the polythene bag and peel by rubbing the skins gently away from the peppers.

Put a layer of red pepper along the base and up the side of the terrine.

Spread a third of the bean purée over the pepper. Cover the purée layer with the aubergine slices and spread over half of the remaining bean purée.

Sprinkle over the basil. Top with the courgettes and the remaining bean purée.

Lay the leeks on top of the purée layer. Add any remaining pieces of pepper. Put a piece of foil, folded four times, on the top and weigh down with cans.

Chill until required. Turn out onto a serving platter, garnish with basil, slice and serve.

serves 4 | prep 40 mins | cook 1 hr 5 mins

aubergines with mozzarella & parmesan

This can be served with a salad as a main course and it also makes a delicious accompaniment to plainly cooked chicken, pork or veal.

INGREDIENTS
3 aubergines, thinly sliced
olive oil, for brushing
300 g/10½ oz mozzarella cheese, sliced
115 g/4 oz freshly grated Parmesan cheese
3 tbsp dried, uncoloured breadcrumbs
1 tbsp butter
salt
fresh flat-leaved parsley sprigs, to garnish

tomato and basil sauce
2 tbsp virgin olive oil
4 shallots, finely chopped
2 garlic cloves, finely chopped
400 g/14 oz canned tomatoes
1 tsp sugar
8 fresh basil leaves, shredded
salt and pepper

Preheat the oven to 200°C/400°F/Gas Mark 6. To remove any bitterness, layer the aubergine slices in a colander, sprinkling each layer with salt. Stand the colander in the sink and leave to drain for 30 minutes. Rinse thoroughly under cold running water to remove all traces of salt, then pat dry with kitchen paper.

Arrange the aubergine slices in a single layer on one or two large baking sheets. Brush with olive oil and bake in the preheated oven for 15–20 minutes, until tender, but not collapsing.

Meanwhile, make the tomato and basil sauce. Heat the oil in a heavy-based saucepan, add the shallots and cook, stirring occasionally, for 5 minutes, until soft. Add the garlic and cook for 1 minute more. Add the tomatoes, with their can juices, and break them up with a wooden spoon. Stir in the sugar and season to taste with salt and pepper. Bring to the boil, reduce the heat and simmer for about 10 minutes, until thickened. Stir in the basil leaves.

Brush an ovenproof dish with olive oil and arrange half the aubergine slices in the base. Cover with half the mozzarella, spoon over half the tomato sauce and sprinkle with half the Parmesan. Mix the remaining Parmesan with the breadcrumbs. Make more layers, ending with the Parmesan mixture.

Dot the top with butter and bake for 25 minutes, until the topping is golden brown. Remove from the oven and leave to stand for 5 minutes before slicing and serving, garnished with parsley.

part four

PANE & PIZZE
bread & pizza

There is an enormous range of different kinds of
bread in Italy, made from a variety of ingredients,
including yeast, olive oil, sun-dried tomatoes,
roasted peppers, olives and herbs. Bread really is
a staple of the Italian diet and is eaten throughout
every meal.

Italians were the inventors of the original
fast food, the pizza – here you will find just some
of the delicious recipes from the almost infinite
variety that can be found in Italian pizzerias.

serves 12 | prep 25 mins + 2 hrs rising | cook 35 mins

black olive focaccia

*Focaccia is an Italian flatbread made
with olive oil. Try serving it with soups
or salads, or on its own as an indulgent
snack at any time of day.*

INGREDIENTS
500 g/1 lb 2 oz strong white flour, plus
   extra for dusting
1 tsp salt
2 tsp easy-blend dried yeast
300 ml/10 fl oz tepid water
90 ml/6 tbsp extra virgin olive oil, plus
   extra for brushing
115 g/4 oz stoned black olives,
   chopped coarsely
1 tsp rock salt

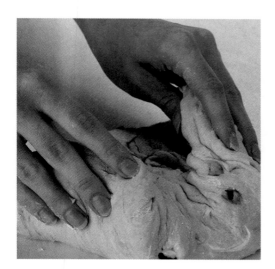

Sift the flour and salt into a warmed bowl and stir in the yeast.
Pour in the water and 2 tablespoons of the olive oil and mix to a
soft dough. Knead the dough on a lightly floured work surface for
5–10 minutes, or until it becomes smooth and elastic. Transfer it to a
clean, warmed, oiled bowl and cover with clingfilm. Leave to stand
in a warm place for 1 hour, or until the dough has doubled in size.

Brush two baking sheets with oil. Knock back the dough to knock
out the air, then knead on a lightly floured work surface for
1 minute. Add the olives and knead until combined. Divide the
dough in half and shape into two ovals 28 x 23 cm/11 x 9 inches
long, and place on the prepared baking trays. Cover with oiled
clingfilm and leave to stand in a warm place for 1 hour, or until
the dough is puffy.

Preheat the oven to 200°C/400°F/Gas Mark 6. Press your fingers
into the dough to make dimples, drizzle over 2 tablespoons of oil
and sprinkle with the rock salt. Bake in the preheated oven for
30–35 minutes, or until golden. Drizzle with the remaining olive oil
and cover with a cloth, to give a soft crust. Slice each loaf into six
pieces and serve warm.

COOK'S TIP
*As the flavour of the olive oil is the
most important part of this bread
recipe, try to use a good-quality,
well-flavoured olive oil.*

serves 4 | prep 15 mins + 45 mins fermenting/rising | cook 30 mins

olive oil bread with cheese

This flat cheese bread is delicious served with antipasto or simply on its own. This recipe makes one loaf.

INGREDIENTS
15 g/½ oz dried yeast
1 tsp sugar
250 ml/9 fl oz hand-hot water
350 g/12 oz strong white flour
1 tsp salt
3 tbsp olive oil
200 g/7 oz pecorino cheese, cubed
½ tbsp fennel seeds, crushed lightly

COOK'S TIP
Pecorino is a hard, quite salty cheese, which is sold in most large supermarkets and Italian delicatessens. If you cannot obtain pecorino, use mature Cheddar or Parmesan cheese instead.

Mix the yeast with the sugar and 8 tablespoons of the water. Leave to ferment in a warm place for about 15 minutes.

Mix the flour with the salt. Add 1 tablespoon of the oil, the yeast mixture and the remaining water to form a smooth dough. Knead the dough for 4 minutes.

Divide the dough into two equal portions. Roll out each portion to form a round 5 mm/¼ inch thick. Place one round on a baking sheet.

Scatter the cheese and half of the fennel seeds evenly over the round of dough.

Place the second round on top and squeeze the edges together to seal so that the filling does not leak during the cooking time.

Using a sharp knife, make a few slashes in the top of the dough and brush with the remaining olive oil.

Sprinkle with the remaining fennel seeds and leave the dough to rise for 20–30 minutes.

Bake in a preheated oven, at 200°C/400°F/Gas Mark 6, for 30 minutes or until golden brown. Serve immediately.

serves 4 | prep 15 mins + 45 mins fermenting/rising | cook 35 mins

sun-dried tomato loaf

This delicious tomato bread is great with cheese or soup or for making an unusual sandwich. This recipe makes one loaf.

INGREDIENTS
7 g/¼ oz dried yeast
1 tsp granulated sugar
300 ml/10 fl oz lukewarm water
450 g/1 lb strong white flour
1 tsp salt
2 tsp dried basil
2 tbsp sun-dried tomato purée
  or tomato purée
margarine, for greasing
12 sun-dried tomatoes in oil, drained
  and cut into strips

Place the yeast and sugar in a bowl and mix with 125 ml/4 fl oz of the water. Let the mixture stand in a warm place to ferment for 15 minutes.

Strain the flour and salt into a bowl. Make a well in the centre and add the basil, yeast mixture, tomato purée and half of the remaining water. Using a wooden spoon, draw the flour into the liquid and mix to form a dough, adding the rest of the water gradually.

Turn out onto a floured work surface and knead for 5 minutes. Cover with oiled clingfilm and let stand in a warm place for 30 minutes or until doubled in size.

Lightly grease a 900-g/2-lb loaf tin with the margarine.

Remove the dough from the bowl and knead in the sun-dried tomatoes. Knead again for 2–3 minutes.

Place the dough in the tin and leave to rise for 30–40 minutes or until it has doubled in size again. Bake in a preheated oven, 190°C/375°F/Gas Mark 5, for 30–35 minutes or until golden and the base sounds hollow when tapped. Cool on a wire rack.

COOK'S TIP
You could make mini sun-dried tomato loaves for children. Divide the dough into 8 equal portions, leave to rise and bake in mini-loaf tins for 20 minutes.

serves 4 | prep 30 mins + 2 hrs rising | cook 40 mins

cheese & potato plait

This bread has a delicious cheese, garlic and rosemary flavour, and is best eaten straight from the oven. This recipe makes a 450-g/1-lb loaf.

INGREDIENTS
175 g/6 oz floury potatoes, diced
2 x 7 g/¼ oz sachets easy-blend
   dried yeast
675 g/1 lb 8 oz strong white flour,
   plus extra for dusting
1 tbsp salt
450 ml/16 fl oz Vegetable Stock (see page 29)
2 garlic cloves, crushed
2 tbsp chopped fresh rosemary
125 g/4½ oz Gruyère cheese, grated
1 tbsp vegetable oil, plus extra for greasing

Lightly grease and flour a baking sheet.

Cook the potatoes in a saucepan of boiling water for 10 minutes or until soft. Drain and mash the potatoes.

Transfer the mashed potatoes to a large mixing bowl.

Stir the yeast, flour, salt and stock into the mashed potatoes and mix together to form a smooth dough.

Add the garlic, rosemary and 75 g/2¾ oz of the cheese and knead the dough for 5 minutes. Make a hollow in the dough, pour in the oil and knead the dough.

Cover the dough and leave to rise in a warm place for 1½ hours or until doubled in

size. Knead the dough again and divide it into three equal portions. Roll each portion into a 35-cm/14-inch sausage shape.

Pressing one end of each of the sausage shapes together, plait the dough and fold the remaining ends underneath. Place the plait on the baking tray, cover and leave to rise for 30 minutes.

Sprinkle the remaining cheese over the top of the plait and bake in a preheated oven, at 190°C/375°F/Gas Mark 5, for 40 minutes or until the base of the loaf sounds hollow when tapped. Serve warm.

serves 4 | prep 1 hr 45 mins | cook 1 hr 5 mins

roasted pepper bread

Peppers become wonderfully sweet and mild when they are roasted, and make this bread delicious.

INGREDIENTS
margarine, for greasing
1 red pepper, halved and deseeded
1 yellow pepper, halved and deseeded
2 sprigs rosemary
1 tbsp olive oil
7 g/¼ oz dried yeast
1 tsp granulated sugar
300 ml/10 fl oz lukewarm water
450 g/1 lb strong white flour
1 tsp salt

Preheat the oven to 200°C/400°F/Gas Mark 6. Grease a 23-cm/9-inch deep circular cake tin with margarine.

Place the red pepper, yellow pepper and rosemary in a shallow roasting tin. Pour over the oil and roast in the preheated oven for 20 minutes, or until slightly charred. Remove the skin from the peppers and cut the flesh into slices.

Place the yeast and sugar in a small bowl and mix with 125 ml/4 fl oz of the water. Set aside in a warm place to ferment for at least 15 minutes.

Sift the flour and salt together into a large bowl. Stir in the yeast mixture and the remaining water and mix to form a smooth dough.

Knead the dough for about 5 minutes until smooth. Cover with oiled clingfilm and leave to rise for 30 minutes or until doubled in size.

Cut the dough into three equal portions. Roll the portions into circles slightly larger than the cake tin.

Place one circle in the base of the tin so that it reaches up the side of the tin by about 2 cm/¾ inch. Top the dough circle with half of the pepper mixture.

Place the second circle of dough on top, followed by the remaining pepper mixture. Place the last circle of dough on top, pushing the edges of the dough down the side of the tin.

Cover the dough with oiled clingfilm and leave to rise for 30–40 minutes. Return to the oven and bake for 45 minutes, or until golden and the base of the loaf sounds hollow when lightly tapped. Transfer to a wire rack to cool slightly, then cut into slices and serve warm.

makes 8 | prep 2 hrs 15 mins | cook 15 mins

sun-dried tomato rolls

These white rolls have the addition of finely chopped sun-dried tomatoes. Use those preserved in jars in olive oil for this recipe.

INGREDIENTS
225 g/8 oz strong white flour, plus extra
   for dusting
½ tsp salt
1 x 7 g/¼ oz sachet easy-blend dried yeast
100 g/3½ oz butter, melted and
   cooled slightly
3 tbsp milk, warmed
2 eggs, beaten
50 g/1¾ oz sun-dried tomatoes, well
   drained and finely chopped
milk, for brushing

Lightly grease a baking tray.

Sift the flour and salt into a large mixing bowl. Stir in the yeast, then pour in the butter, milk and eggs. Mix together to form a dough.

Turn the dough onto a lightly floured work surface and knead for about 5 minutes

Place the dough in a greased bowl, cover and leave to rise in a warm place for 1–1½ hours or until the dough has doubled in size. Knock back the dough for approximately 2–3 minutes.

Knead the sun-dried tomatoes into the dough, sprinkling the work surface with extra flour as the tomatoes are quite oily.

Divide the dough into eight balls and place them on the baking sheet. Cover and leave to rise for about 30 minutes or until the rolls have doubled in size.

Brush the rolls with milk and bake in a preheated oven, 230°C/450°F/Gas Mark 8, for 10–15 minutes, until golden brown.

Transfer the rolls to a wire rack and cool slightly before serving.

makes 8 | prep 1 hr 45 mins | cook 35 mins

garlic bread rolls

This bread is not at all like the store-bought, ready-made garlic bread. Instead it has a subtle flavour and a soft texture.

INGREDIENTS
butter, for greasing
12 cloves garlic, peeled
350 ml/12 fl oz milk
450 g/1 lb strong white flour
1 tsp salt
1 x 7 g/¼ oz sachet easy-blend dried yeast
1 tbsp dried mixed herbs
45 ml/3 tbsp sunflower oil
1 egg, beaten lightly
milk, for brushing
rock salt, for sprinkling

Grease a baking tray with a little butter and set aside.

Place the garlic cloves and milk in a saucepan, bring to the boil and simmer gently for 15 minutes. Cool slightly, then process in a blender or food processor to blend in the garlic.

Sift the flour and salt into a large mixing bowl, stir in the yeast, then add the mixed herbs to the mixture.

Add the garlic-flavoured milk, sunflower oil and beaten egg to the dry ingredients and mix to form a dough.

Place the dough on a lightly floured work surface and knead lightly for a few minutes until smooth and soft.

Place the dough in a greased bowl, cover and leave to rise in a warm place for about 1 hour or until doubled in size.

Knead the dough for 2 minutes. Divide the dough into eight pieces and shape into rolls. Score the tops of the rolls with a knife and place them on the baking sheet. Cover and leave to stand for 15 minutes.

Brush the rolls with milk and sprinkle rock salt over the top. Bake in a preheated oven, 220°C/425°F/Gas Mark 7, for 15–20 minutes.

Transfer the rolls to a wire rack to cool before serving.

makes 2 | prep 10 mins | cook 20 mins

pizza margherita

*With its red, white and green ingredients –
the colours of the Italian flag – this
pizza was created to honour Queen
Margherita. While it is delicious with just
this simple topping, it can also be used
as a basis for more elaborate pizzas with
extra ingredients.*

INGREDIENTS
**1 quantity Basic Pizza Dough
  (see page 24)**

topping
6 tomatoes, thinly sliced
**175 g/6 oz mozzarella cheese, drained
  and sliced thinly**
2 tbsp shredded fresh basil leaves
2 tbsp olive oil
salt and pepper

Turn out the Basic Pizza Dough onto a lightly floured work surface
and knock back. Knead briefly, then cut it in half and roll out each
piece into a circle about 5 mm/¼ inch thick.

Transfer to a lightly oiled baking sheet and push up the edges with
your fingers to form a small rim.

For the topping, arrange the tomato and mozzarella slices alternately
over the pizza bases. Season to taste with salt and pepper, sprinkle
with the basil and drizzle with the olive oil.

Bake in a preheated oven, 230°C/450°F/Gas Mark 8, for 15–20
minutes, until the cheese has melted. Serve immediately.

VARIATION
*For Pizza Napoletana, first spread each
pizza base with 4½ teaspoons tomato
purée, then top with the tomato and
cheese slices. Arrange halved, drained,
canned anchovy fillets in a pattern on
top, season to taste with pepper, drizzle
with olive oil and bake as above.*

makes 1 | prep 1 hr 15 mins | cook 30 mins

tomato & ricotta pizza

This is a traditional dish from the Calabrian Mountains in southern Italy, where it is made with naturally sun-dried tomatoes and ricotta cheese.

INGREDIENTS
1 quantity Basic Pizza Dough (see page 24)
olive oil, for greasing
flour, for dusting

topping
4 tbsp sun-dried tomato purée
150 g/5½ oz ricotta cheese
10 sun-dried tomatoes in oil, drained
1 tbsp fresh thyme
salt and pepper

Preheat the oven to 200°C/400°F/Gas Mark 6. Knead the Basic Pizza Dough on a lightly floured work surface for 2 minutes.

Using a rolling pin, roll out the dough to form a circle, then carefully transfer it to an oiled baking sheet, pushing out the edges until even. The dough should be no more than about 5 mm/¼ inch thick because it will rise during cooking.

Spread the sun-dried tomato purée evenly over the dough, then add spoonfuls of ricotta cheese, dotting them over the pizza.

Cut the sun-dried tomatoes into strips and arrange these on top of the pizza.

Sprinkle the thyme over the top of the pizza and season with salt and pepper to taste. Bake in the preheated oven for 30 minutes or until piping hot with a golden crust. Serve immediately.

makes 1 | prep 1 hr 15 mins | cook 40 mins

onion, prosciutto & cheese pizza

This pizza is a favourite of the Romans. It is slightly unusual because the topping is made without a tomato sauce base.

INGREDIENTS
1 quantity Basic Pizza Dough (see page 24)
olive oil, for greasing
flour, for dusting

topping
2 tbsp olive oil
250 g/9 oz onions,
  sliced into rings
2 garlic cloves, crushed
1 red pepper, diced
100 g/3½ oz prosciutto,
  cut into strips
100 g/3½ oz mozzarella cheese, sliced
2 tbsp rosemary, stalks removed and
  roughly chopped

Preheat the oven to 200°C/400°F/Gas Mark 6. Lightly grease a baking sheet. Turn out the Basic Pizza Dough onto a lightly floured work surface and knock back. Knead on a lightly floured work surface for 2 minutes.

Using a rolling pin, roll out the dough to form a square shape, then place it on the prepared baking sheet, pushing out the edges until even. The dough should be no more than 5 mm/¼ inch thick because it will rise during cooking.

To make the topping, heat the oil in a frying pan. Add the onions and garlic and cook for 3 minutes. Add the red pepper and fry for 2 minutes. Cover the pan and cook over a low heat for 10 minutes, stirring occasionally, until the onions are slightly caramelized. Leave to cool slightly.

Spread the topping evenly over the pizza base. Arrange the prosciutto, cheese and rosemary over the top.

Bake the pizza in the preheated oven for 20–25 minutes. Serve immediately.

VARIATION
To ring the changes with this pizza, use cooked ham (prosciutto cotto) instead of the prosciutto and add 70 g/2½ oz button mushrooms to the onion and garlic mixture before adding the pepper. Use red onions instead of white to add extra colour to the pizza.

makes 1 | prep 1 hr 15 mins | cook 45 mins

mushroom pizza

Juicy mushrooms and stringy mozzarella top this tomato-based pizza. Use wild mushrooms or a combination of wild and cultivated mushrooms.

INGREDIENTS
1 quantity Basic Pizza Dough (see page 24)
olive oil, for greasing
flour, for dusting

topping
400 g/14 oz canned chopped tomatoes
2 garlic cloves, crushed
1 tsp dried basil
1 tbsp olive oil
2 tbsp tomato purée
200 g/7 oz mushrooms, thinly sliced
150 g/5½ oz grated mozzarella cheese
salt and pepper
fresh basil leaves, to garnish

Preheat the oven to 200°C/400°F/Gas Mark 6. Lightly grease a baking sheet. Knead the Basic Pizza Dough on a lightly floured work surface for 2 minutes.

Using a rolling pin, roll out the dough to form an oval or a circular shape, then place it on the prepared baking sheet, pushing out the edges until even. The dough should be no more than 5 mm/¼ inch thick because it will rise during cooking.

To make the topping, place the tomatoes, garlic, dried basil, oil, and salt and pepper to taste in a large saucepan and simmer for 20 minutes.

Stir in the tomato purée and leave the sauce to cool slightly.

Spread the sauce over the base of the pizza, top with the mushrooms and scatter over the cheese.

Bake the pizza in the preheated oven for 25 minutes, until the cheese is melted. Garnish with basil leaves and serve immediately.

makes 1 | prep 1 hr 45 mins | cook 20 mins

cheese & artichoke pizza

Sliced artichoke hearts combined with mature Cheddar, tangy Parmesan and blue cheese give a really delicious topping to this pizza.

INGREDIENTS
1 quantity Basic Pizza Dough (see page 24)
olive oil, for greasing
flour, for dusting
salad leaves and cherry tomatoes,
    halved, to serve

topping
Basic Tomato Sauce (see page 26)
60 g/2 oz blue cheese, sliced
125 g/4½ oz artichoke hearts in oil, sliced,
    oil reserved
½ small red onion, chopped
45 g/1½ oz grated mature Cheddar cheese
2 tbsp freshly grated Parmesan cheese
1 tbsp chopped fresh thyme
salt and pepper

Preheat the oven to 200°C/400°F/Gas Mark 6. Lightly grease a baking sheet. Roll out or press the dough, using a rolling pin or your hands, to form a 25-cm/10-inch circle on a lightly floured work surface.

Place the pizza base on the prepared baking sheet and push up the edge slightly. Cover and leave to rise for 10 minutes in a warm place.

Spread the tomato sauce almost to the edge of the base. Arrange the blue cheese on top of the sauce, followed by the artichoke hearts and red onion.

Mix the Cheddar cheese and Parmesan cheese together with the thyme and sprinkle the mixture over the pizza. Drizzle over a little of the reserved artichoke oil and season to taste with salt and pepper.

Bake the pizza in the preheated oven for 18–20 minutes, until the cheese is bubbling.

Mix the fresh salad leaves and cherry tomato halves together and serve with the pizza, cut into slices.

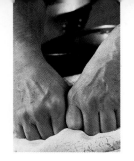

makes 1 | prep 1 hr 45 mins | cook 1 hr

four seasons pizza

This pizza is divided into four sections, each with a different topping, to represent the four seasons. You can vary the toppings according to taste.

INGREDIENTS
1 quantity Basic Pizza Dough (see page 24)
olive oil, for greasing
flour, for dusting

tomato sauce
2 tbsp olive oil
1 small onion, finely chopped
1 garlic clove, finely chopped
1 red pepper, deseeded and chopped
225 g/8 oz plum tomatoes, peeled
   (see Cook's Tip, page 111) and chopped
1 tbsp tomato purée
1 tsp demerara sugar
1 tbsp shredded fresh basil leaves
1 bay leaf
salt and pepper

topping
70 g/2½ oz drained bottled clams or drained
   anchovy fillets, halved lengthways, or
   cooked peeled prawns
55 g/2 oz baby globe artichokes or artichoke
   hearts, thinly sliced, or canned asparagus
   spears, drained
25 g/1 oz mozzarella cheese, drained and
   thinly sliced
1 tomato, thinly sliced
100 g/3½ oz mushrooms or pepperoni,
   thinly sliced
2 tsp capers, rinsed
2 tsp stoned, sliced black olives
2 tbsp olive oil, plus extra for brushing
salt and pepper

To make the tomato sauce, heat the olive oil in a heavy-based saucepan. Add the onion, garlic and pepper, and cook over a low heat, stirring occasionally, for 5 minutes, until soft. Add the tomatoes, tomato purée, sugar, basil and bay leaf, and season to taste with salt and pepper. Cover and simmer, stirring occasionally, for 30 minutes, until thickened. Remove the saucepan from the heat and let the sauce cool completely.

Preheat the oven to 220°C/425°F/Gas Mark 7. Lightly grease a baking sheet. Turn out the prepared pizza dough onto a lightly floured work surface and knock back. Knead briefly, then cut it in half and roll out each piece into a circle about 5 mm/¼ inch thick. Transfer to the prepared baking sheet and push up the edges with your fingers to form a small rim.

Spread the tomato sauce over the pizza bases, almost to the edge. Cover one-quarter with clams. Cover a second quarter with sliced artichokes. Cover the third quarter with alternate slices of cheese and tomato. Cover the final quarter with sliced mushrooms. Sprinkle the surface with capers and olives, season to taste with salt and pepper and drizzle with olive oil.

Bake the pizza in the preheated oven for 20–25 minutes, until the cheese has melted. Serve immediately.

VARIATION
Other toppings, either used in combination or singly, could include: mixed seafood, such as prawns, mussels and squid rings; roasted Mediterranean vegetables, say aubergines, peppers, tomatoes, courgettes and red onions; exotic mushrooms and pine kernels; or hot pepperoni and chillies.

makes 1 | prep 20 mins | cook 55 mins

pissaladière

This is a variation of the classic Italian pizza but is made with ready-made pastry. It is perfect for outdoor eating.

Lightly grease a swiss roll tin. Heat the olive oil in a large saucepan. Add the red onions and garlic and cook over a low heat for about 30 minutes, stirring occasionally.

Add the sugar and vinegar to the pan and season with plenty of salt and pepper.

Preheat the oven to 220°C/425°F/Gas Mark 7. On a lightly floured work surface, roll out the pastry to a rectangle 13 x 23 cm/ 5 x 9 inches. Place the pastry rectangle onto the prepared tin, pushing the pastry into the corners of the tin.

Spread the onion mixture over the pastry. Arrange the anchovy fillets and olives on top, then sprinkle over the marjoram.

Bake the pissaladière in the preheated oven for 20–25 minutes, or until golden. Serve piping hot, straight from the oven.

INGREDIENTS
60 ml/4 tbsp olive oil, plus extra for greasing
700 g/1 lb 9 oz red onions, thinly sliced
2 garlic cloves, crushed
2 tsp caster sugar
2 tbsp red wine vinegar
flour, for dusting
350 g/12 oz puff pastry, thawed if frozen
salt and pepper

topping
100 g/3½ oz canned anchovy fillets
12 stoned green olives
1 tsp dried marjoram

COOK'S TIP
Cut the pissaladière into squares or triangles for easy finger food at a party or barbecue.

makes 4 | prep 1 hr 30 mins | cook 40 mins

vegetable calzone

These pizza base parcels are great for making in advance and freezing – they can be defrosted when required for a quick snack.

INGREDIENTS
dough
450 g/1 lb strong white flour, plus extra for dusting
2 tsp easy-blend dried yeast
1 tsp caster sugar
175 ml/6 fl oz Vegetable Stock (see page 29)
175 ml/6 fl oz passata
olive oil, for greasing
beaten egg

filling
1 tbsp vegetable oil
1 onion, chopped
1 garlic clove, crushed
2 tbsp chopped sun-dried tomatoes
100 g/3½ oz spinach, chopped
3 tbsp canned and drained sweetcorn
25 g/1 oz French beans, cut into 2.5-cm/ 1-inch pieces
1 tbsp tomato purée
1 tbsp chopped oregano
50 g/1¾ oz mozzarella cheese, sliced
salt and pepper

Sift the flour into a bowl. Add the yeast and sugar and beat in the stock and passata to make a smooth dough.

Knead the dough on a lightly floured work surface for 10 minutes, then place in a clean, lightly oiled bowl and leave to rise in a warm place for 1 hour.

Preheat the oven to 220°C/425°F/Gas Mark 7. Lightly grease a baking sheet.

To make the filling, heat the oil in a frying pan, add the onion and sauté for 2–3 minutes. Stir in the garlic, tomatoes, spinach, sweetcorn and beans and cook for 3–4 minutes. Add the tomato purée and oregano and season with salt and pepper.

Divide the dough into four equal portions and roll out each on a floured work surface to form an 18-cm/7-inch circle. Spoon a quarter of the filling onto one half of each circle and top with cheese. Fold the dough over to encase the filling, sealing the edge with a fork. Glaze with beaten egg, place on the prepared baking sheet and bake in the preheated oven for 25–30 minutes, until risen and golden. Serve warm.

makes 4 | prep 1 hr 30 mins | cook 35 mins

potato & tomato calzone

These pizza dough Italian pasties are best served hot with a salad as a delicious lunch or supper dish.

INGREDIENTS
dough
500 g/1 lb 2 oz strong white flour, plus extra for dusting
1 tsp easy-blend dried yeast
300 ml/10 fl oz Vegetable Stock (see page 29)
1 tbsp clear honey
1 tsp caraway seeds
olive oil, for greasing
milk, for glazing

filling
1 tbsp vegetable oil
225 g/8 oz waxy potatoes, diced
1 onion, halved and sliced
2 garlic cloves, crushed
40 g/1½ oz sun-dried tomatoes
2 tbsp chopped fresh basil
2 tbsp tomato purée
2 celery sticks, sliced
50 g/1¾ oz grated mozzarella cheese

Lightly grease a baking sheet. To make the dough, sift the flour into a large bowl and stir in the yeast. Make a well in the centre of the mixture.

Stir in the vegetable stock, honey and caraway seeds and bring the mixture together to form a dough.

Turn the dough out onto a lightly floured work surface and knead for 8 minutes until smooth. Place the dough in a lightly oiled mixing bowl, cover and leave to rise in a warm place for 1 hour or until it has doubled in size.

Preheat the oven to 220°C/425°F/Gas Mark 7. Meanwhile, make the filling. Heat the oil in a frying pan and add all of the remaining ingredients except for the cheese. Cook for 5 minutes, stirring constantly.

Divide the risen dough into four pieces. On a lightly floured work surface, roll them out to form four 18-cm/7-inch circles. Spoon equal amounts of the filling onto one half of each circle.

Sprinkle the cheese over the filling. Brush the edges of the dough with milk and fold the dough over to form four semi-circles, pressing to seal the edges.

Place on the prepared baking sheet and brush with milk. Bake in the preheated oven for 30 minutes, until golden and risen. Serve hot.

makes 1 | prep 1 hr 30 mins | cook 25 mins

seafood pizza

Bags of fresh mixed seafood, containing prawns, squid rings, mussels and other shellfish are available from the chiller cabinets of many supermarkets. These tend to have a better flavour and texture than frozen seafood.

INGREDIENTS
1 quantity Basic Pizza Dough (see page 24)
olive oil, for greasing and drizzling
flour, for dusting

topping
1 quantity Basic Tomato Sauce (see page 26)
225 g/8 oz mixed fresh* seafood
½ red pepper, deseeded and chopped
½ yellow pepper, deseeded and chopped
1 tbsp capers, rinsed
55 g/2 oz Taleggio cheese
3 tbsp freshly grated Parmesan cheese
½ tsp dried oregano
**75 g/2¾ oz anchovy fillets in oil,
   drained and sliced**
10 black olives, stoned
salt and pepper

Preheat the oven to 220°C/425°F/Gas Mark 7. Lightly grease a baking sheet. Turn out the Basic Pizza Dough onto a lightly floured work surface and knock back. Knead briefly, then roll out the dough into a circle about 5 mm/¼ inch thick. Transfer to the prepared baking sheet and push up the edge with your fingers to form a small rim.

Spread the tomato sauce over the pizza base, almost to the edge. Arrange the mixed seafood, red peppers, yellow peppers and capers evenly on top. Sprinkle the Taleggio cheese, Parmesan cheese and oregano evenly over the topping. Add the anchovy fillets and olives, drizzle with oil and season to taste with salt and pepper.

Bake the pizza in the preheated oven for 20–25 minutes, until the cheese has melted. Serve immediately.

COOK'S TIP
*If you have to use frozen mixed seafood, make sure that it is completely thawed first.

makes 8 | prep 1 hr 15 mins | cook 15 mins

mini pizzas

Pizzette, as they are known in Italy, are tiny pizzas. This quantity will make eight individual pizzas, or 16 cocktail pizzas to go with drinks.

INGREDIENTS
1 quantity Basic Pizza Dough (see page 24)
olive oil, for greasing
flour, for dusting

topping
2 courgettes
100 g/3½ oz passata
75 g/2¾ oz pancetta,* diced
50 g/1¾ oz black olives,* stoned and chopped
1 tbsp mixed dried herbs
2 tbsp olive oil
salt and pepper

Preheat the oven to 220°C/425°F/Gas Mark 7. Lightly grease a baking sheet. Turn out the Basic Pizza Dough onto a lightly floured work surface and knock back. Knead the dough for 2 minutes and divide it into eight balls.

Roll out each portion thinly to form circles or squares, then place them on the prepared baking sheet, pushing out the edges until even. The dough should be no more than 5 mm/¼ inch thick because it will rise during cooking.

To make the topping, finely grate the courgettes. Cover with kitchen paper and leave to stand for 10 minutes to absorb some of the juices. Spread 2–3 teaspoons of the passata over the pizza bases and top with the grated courgettes, pancetta and olives.

Season to taste with pepper, sprinkle with mixed dried herbs and drizzle with olive oil.

Bake the pizzas in the preheated oven for 15 minutes, or until crispy. Season to taste with salt and pepper and serve hot.

VARIATIONS
*You can use smoked pancetta if you want your pizzas to have a more intense flavour. Green olives can be substituted for the stronger-tasting black olives, although the pizzas will have less colour contrast.

part five

DOLCI
desserts, cakes & biscuits

Creamy or fruity desserts, tarts, cakes, ice creams,

sorbets and biscuits are the grand finale in the

Italian menu. They are usually served only on

special occasions but you should always be able to

find an excuse for making one of the delicious

sweet creations found here!

serves 4 | prep 5 mins | cook 15 mins

zabaglione

This well-known dish is really a light but rich egg mousse flavoured with Marsala.

INGREDIENTS
5 egg yolks
100 g/3½ oz caster sugar
150 ml/5 fl oz Marsala or
  sweet sherry
amaretti biscuits, to serve
  (optional)

Place the egg yolks in a large mixing bowl.

Add the caster sugar to the egg yolks and whisk until the mixture is thick and very pale and has doubled in volume.

Place the bowl containing the egg yolk and sugar mixture over a pan of gently simmering water.

Add the Marsala or sherry to the egg yolk and sugar mixture and continue whisking until the foam mixture becomes warm. This process may take as long as 10 minutes.

Pour the mixture, which should be frothy and light, into four wine glasses.

Serve the zabaglione warm with amaretti biscuits, if you wish.

serves 6 | prep 25 mins + 8 hrs chilling | cook 10 mins

coffee panna cotta with chocolate sauce

Panna cotta literally means 'cooked cream'. Flavouring it with coffee and serving it with a chocolate sauce adds a new look to this popular Italian dessert.

INGREDIENTS
oil, for brushing
600 ml/1 pint double cream
1 vanilla pod
55 g/2 oz golden caster sugar
2 tsp instant espresso coffee granules, dissolved in 4 tbsp water
2 tsp powdered gelatine
chocolate-covered coffee beans, to serve
cocoa powder, for dusting

sauce
150 ml/5 fl oz single cream
55 g/2 oz plain chocolate, melted

Lightly brush 6 x 150-ml/5 fl oz moulds with oil. Place the cream in a saucepan. Split the vanilla pod and scrape the black seeds into the cream. Add the vanilla pod and the sugar, then heat gently until almost boiling. Strain the cream into a heatproof bowl and set aside. Place the coffee in a small heatproof bowl, sprinkle on the gelatine and let stand for 5 minutes, or until spongy. Set the bowl over a saucepan of gently simmering water until the gelatine has dissolved.

Stir a little of the reserved cream into the gelatine mixture, then stir the gelatine mixture into the remainder of the cream.

Divide the mixture between the prepared moulds and leave to cool, then chill in the refrigerator for 8 hours, or overnight.

To make the sauce, place a quarter of the cream in a bowl and stir in the melted chocolate. Gradually stir in the remaining cream, reserving 1 tablespoon. Dip the base of the moulds briefly into hot water and turn out onto six dessert plates. Pour the chocolate cream around. Dot drops of the reserved cream onto the sauce and feather with a cocktail stick. Decorate with chocolate-covered coffee beans, dust with cocoa powder and serve.

serves 8 | prep 30 mins + 3 hrs chilling | cook 30 mins

tiramisù

Tiramisù is an Italian version of the British trifle. A wicked combination of mascarpone, chocolate, coffee and rum makes this delicious dessert very rich and quite irresistible!

INGREDIENTS
butter, for greasing
3 eggs
140 g/5 oz golden caster sugar
90 g/3¼ oz self-raising flour
1 tbsp cocoa powder
150 ml/5 fl oz cold black coffee
2 tbsp rum
2 tsp cocoa powder, to decorate

filling
375g/13 oz mascarpone cheese
225 ml/8 fl oz fresh custard
55 g/2 oz golden caster sugar
100 g/3½ oz plain
   chocolate, grated

Preheat the oven to 180°C/350°F/Gas Mark 4. To make the cake, grease a 20-cm/8-inch round cake tin with butter and line with baking paper. Place the eggs and sugar in a large bowl and beat together until thick and light. Sift the flour and cocoa powder over the batter and fold in gently. Spoon the batter into the prepared tin and bake in the oven for 30 minutes, or until the cake springs back when pressed gently in the centre. Leave to stand in the tin for 5 minutes, then turn out onto a wire rack.

Place the black coffee and rum in a bowl or cup, mix together and set aside. To make the filling, place the mascarpone in a large bowl and beat until soft. Stir in the custard, then gradually add the sugar, beating constantly. Stir in the grated chocolate.

Cut the cake horizontally into three layers and place one layer on a serving plate. Sprinkle with one-third of the coffee mixture, then cover with one-third of the mascarpone mixture. Repeat the layers, finishing with a topping of the mascarpone mixture. Chill in the refrigerator for 3 hours. Sift over the cocoa powder before serving.

VARIATION
To save time, use sponge fingers instead of cake. Dip the sponge fingers in coffee and layer them with the mascarpone mixture in a bowl.

serves 6 | prep 1 hr + 1 hr chilling | cook 50 mins

pear tart

Pears are a very popular fruit in Italy. In this recipe from Trentino they are flavoured with almonds, cinnamon, raisins and apricot jam.

INGREDIENTS
275 g/9¾ oz plain flour
pinch of salt
125 g/4½ oz caster sugar
125 g/4½ oz butter, diced, plus extra
   for greasing
1 egg
1 egg yolk
few drops of vanilla extract
2–3 tsp water
sifted icing sugar, for sprinkling

filling
4 tbsp apricot jam
60 g/2¼ oz amaretti biscuits, crumbled
850 g–1 kg/1 lb 4 oz–2 lb 4 oz pears,
   peeled and cored
1 tsp ground cinnamon
90 g/3¼ oz raisins
60 g/2¼ oz demerara sugar

Sift the flour and salt onto a flat surface, make a well in the centre and add the sugar, butter, egg, egg yolk, vanilla extract and most of the water.

Using your fingers, gradually work the flour into the other ingredients to give a smooth dough, adding more water if necessary. Wrap in clingfilm and chill until firm (about 1 hour). Alternatively, put all the ingredients into a food processor and work until smooth.

Preheat the oven to 200°C/400°F/ Gas Mark 6. Grease a shallow 25-cm/ 10-inch cake tin or deep flan tin. Roll out three-quarters of the pastry and use to line the prepared tin. Spread the jam over the base and sprinkle with the crushed biscuits.

Slice the pears very thinly. Arrange over the biscuits in the pastry case. Sprinkle with cinnamon, then with raisins and, finally, with brown sugar.

Roll out a thin sausage shape using one-third of the remaining pastry, and place around the edge of the pie. Roll the remainder into thin sausages and arrange in a lattice over the tart, four or five strips in each direction, attaching them to the strip around the edge.

Bake in the preheated oven for 50 minutes, or until golden and cooked through. Leave to cool, then serve warm or chilled, lightly sprinkled with sifted icing sugar.

serves 6–8 | prep 1 hr + 30 mins chilling | cook 55 mins

ricotta cheesecake

This melt-in-the-mouth cheesecake confirms the belief that all the best Italian desserts come from Sicily.

INGREDIENTS
pastry
275 g/9¾ oz plain flour, plus extra
   for dusting
3 tbsp caster sugar
salt
115 g/4 oz unsalted butter,
   chilled and diced
1 egg yolk

filling
450 g/1 lb ricotta cheese
125 ml/4 fl oz double cream
2 eggs, plus 1 egg yolk
85 g/3 oz caster sugar
finely grated rind of 1 lemon
finely grated rind of 1 orange

To make the pastry, sift the flour with the sugar and a pinch of salt onto a work surface and make a well in the centre. Add the butter and egg yolk and, using your fingertips, gradually work in the flour mixture until fully incorporated.

Grease a 23-cm/9-inch tart tin and line with baking paper. Gather up the pastry and knead very lightly.

Cut off about one quarter of the kneaded pastry, wrap in clingfilm and chill in the refrigerator. Press the remaining pastry into the base of the prepared tart tin and chill for 30 minutes.

Preheat the oven to 190°C/375°F/Gas Mark 5. To make the filling, beat the ricotta cheese with the cream, eggs and egg yolk, sugar, lemon rind and orange rind. Cover with clingfilm and set aside in the refrigerator until needed.

Prick the base of the pastry case all over with a fork. Line with foil, fill with baking beans and bake blind in the preheated oven for 15 minutes. Remove from the oven and take out the foil and baking beans. Stand the tin on a wire rack and set aside.

Spoon the ricotta mixture into the pastry case and level the surface. Roll out the reserved pastry on a lightly floured work surface and cut it into strips. Arrange the strips over the filling in a lattice pattern, brushing the overlapping ends with water so that they stick.

Return the cheesecake to the oven and bake for 30–35 minutes, until the top is golden and the filling has set. Leave to cool on a wire rack before lifting off the side of the tin. Cut into wedges to serve.

serves 6 | prep 15 mins + 3-48 hrs chilling | cook 20 mins

caramelized oranges

The secret of these oranges is to allow them to marinate in the syrup for at least 24 hours, so the flavours amalgamate.

INGREDIENTS
6 large oranges
225 g/8 oz sugar
225 ml/8 fl oz water
6 whole cloves (optional)
**2-4 tbsp orange-flavoured liqueur
   or brandy**

Using a citrus zester or potato peeler, pare the rind from two of the oranges in narrow strips without any white pith attached. If using a potato peeler, cut the peel into very thin julienne strips.

Put the orange strips into a small saucepan and barely cover with water. Bring to the boil and simmer for 5 minutes. Drain the strips and reserve the water.

Cut away all the white pith and peel from the remaining oranges using a very sharp knife, then cut horizontally into four slices. Reassemble the oranges and hold in place with cocktail sticks. Stand in an ovenproof dish.

Put the sugar and water into a heavy-based saucepan with the cloves, if using. Bring to the boil and simmer gently until the sugar has dissolved, then boil hard without stirring until the syrup thickens and begins to colour. Continue to cook until a light golden brown, then quickly remove from the heat and carefully pour in the reserved orange rind liquid.

Place over a gentle heat until the caramel has fully dissolved again, then remove from the heat and add the liqueur or brandy. Pour the syrup over the oranges.

Sprinkle the orange strips over the oranges, cover with clingfilm and leave to stand until cold. Chill for at least 3 hours and preferably for 24-48 hours before serving. If time allows, spoon the syrup over the oranges several times while they are marinating. Discard the cocktail sticks before serving.

serves 4 | prep 20 mins + 1 hr 20 mins chilling | cook 0 mins

sweet mascarpone mousse

This sweet cream cheese dessert is a perfect complement to the tartness of fresh summer fruits.

INGREDIENTS
450 g/1 lb mascarpone cheese
4 egg yolks
100 g/3½ oz caster sugar
400 g/14 oz frozen summer fruits, such as raspberries and redcurrants
redcurrants, to garnish
amaretti biscuits, to serve

Place the mascarpone in a large mixing bowl. Using a wooden spoon, beat the mascarpone until quite smooth.

Stir the egg yolks and sugar into the mascarpone, mixing well. Chill the mixture in the refrigerator for 1 hour.

Spoon a layer of the mascarpone mixture into the bottom of four individual serving dishes. Spoon a layer of the summer fruits on top of the mixture. Repeat the layers in the same order, reserving some of the mascarpone mixture for the top.

Leave the mousses to chill in the refrigerator for about 20 minutes. The fruits should still be slightly frozen.

Garnish the mousses with redcurrants and serve with amaretti biscuits.

serves 4 | prep 15 mins + 30 mins chilling | cook 25 mins

italian bread pudding

This deliciously rich pudding is cooked with cream and apples and is delicately flavoured with orange.

INGREDIENTS
1 tbsp butter
2 small eating apples, peeled, cored and
    sliced into rings
75 g/2¾ oz granulated sugar
2 tbsp white wine
100 g/3½ oz white bread, sliced, with
    crusts removed (slightly stale French
    baguette is ideal)
300 ml/10 fl oz single cream
2 eggs, beaten
pared rind of 1 orange, cut into short strips

Lightly grease a 1.2-litre/2-pint deep oven-proof dish with the butter.

Arrange the apple rings in the base of the dish. Sprinkle half of the sugar evenly over the apples.

Pour the wine over the apples. Add the bread slices, pushing them down with your hands to flatten them slightly.

Mix the cream with the eggs, the remaining sugar and the orange rind and pour the mixture over the bread. Leave to soak for 30 minutes.

Bake the pudding in a preheated oven, 180°C/350°F/Gas Mark 4, for 25 minutes until golden and set. Serve warm.

makes 16 | prep 30 mins + 1 hr rising | cook 20 mins

baked sweet ravioli

These scrumptious little parcels are the perfect dessert for anyone with a really sweet tooth.

INGREDIENTS
sweet pasta dough
425 g/15 oz plain flour, plus extra
   for dusting
140 g/5 oz butter, plus extra
   for greasing
140 g/5 oz caster sugar
4 eggs
25 g/1 oz yeast
125 ml/4 fl oz warm milk

filling
175 g/6 oz chestnut purée
60 g/2¼ oz cocoa powder
60 g/2¼ oz caster sugar
60 g/2¼ oz chopped almonds
60 g/2¼ oz crushed amaretti biscuits
175 g/6 oz orange marmalade

To make the sweet pasta dough, sift the flour into a mixing bowl, then mix in the butter, sugar and 3 eggs.

Mix the yeast and warm milk together in a small bowl and, when thoroughly combined, mix into the dough.

Knead the dough for 20 minutes, cover with a clean cloth and set aside in a warm place for 1 hour to rise.

To make the filling, mix the chestnut purée, cocoa powder, sugar, almonds, crushed amaretti biscuits and orange marmalade together in a separate bowl.

Preheat the oven to 180°C/350°F/Gas Mark 4. Grease a baking sheet with butter.

Lightly flour a work surface. Roll out the pasta dough into a thin sheet and cut into 5-cm/2-inch rounds with a plain pastry cutter.

Put a spoonful of filling onto each round and then fold in half, pressing the edges to seal. Arrange on the prepared baking sheet, spacing the ravioli out well.

Beat the remaining egg and brush all over the ravioli to glaze. Bake in the preheated oven for 20 minutes. Serve hot.

serves 4 | prep 20 mins + 1–2 hrs chilling | cook 0 mins

mascarpone creams

Rich and self-indulgent, these creamy desserts make the perfect end to a special-occasion meal.

INGREDIENTS
115 g/4 oz amaretti biscuits, crushed*
90 ml/6 tbsp amaretto or maraschino
4 eggs, separated
55 g/2 oz caster sugar
225 g/8 oz mascarpone cheese
toasted flaked almonds, to decorate

Place the amaretti crumbs in a bowl, add the amaretto or maraschino and set aside to soak.

Meanwhile, beat the egg yolks with the sugar until pale and thick. Fold in the mascarpone and soaked biscuit crumbs.

Whisk the egg whites in a separate, spotlessly clean, bowl until stiff, then gently fold into the cheese mixture. Divide the mascarpone cream between four serving dishes and chill for 1–2 hours. Sprinkle with toasted flaked almonds just before serving.

COOK'S TIP
*The easiest way to make biscuit crumbs is to place the biscuits in a plastic bag and crush them with a rolling pin.

serves 6 | prep 20 mins | cook 30 mins

stuffed peaches

Peaches grow throughout central and southern Italy – in fact this recipe comes from Piedmont in the northwest.

INGREDIENTS
55 g/2 oz unsalted butter, plus extra for
  greasing
6 large peaches*
25 g/1 oz ground almonds
55 g/2 oz amaretti biscuits, crushed coarsely
1 tbsp amaretto
½ tsp grated lemon rind
1 tsp cocoa powder
2 tsp icing sugar
225 ml/8 fl oz medium-dry white wine

Preheat the oven to 180°C/350°F/Gas
Mark 4. Grease an ovenproof dish with
butter. Cut the peaches in half and remove
and discard the stones. Widen the central
cavity by cutting away and reserving some
of the flesh in a bowl.

Add the almonds, amaretti, amaretto, lemon
rind and half the butter to the reserved
peach flesh and mash with a fork. Fill the
peach cavities with this mixture and place
them in the dish.

Dot the peaches with the remaining butter
and sprinkle with the cocoa powder and
icing sugar. Pour the wine into the dish and
bake in the preheated oven for 30 minutes,
until golden. Serve immediately.

COOK'S TIP
Use white peaches if you can find them, as they have the sweetest, most succulent flavour. White or yellow, do make sure the peaches are really ripe.

serves 4 | prep 35 mins | cook 2 mins

panettone & strawberries

Panettone is a sweet Italian bread. It is delicious toasted, and when it is topped with mascarpone and strawberries it makes a sumptuous dessert.

INGREDIENTS
225 g/8 oz strawberries
25 g/1 oz caster sugar
6 tbsp Marsala
½ tsp ground cinnamon
4 slices panettone
4 tbsp mascarpone cheese

Hull and slice the strawberries and place them in a bowl. Add the sugar, Marsala and cinnamon to the strawberries.

Toss the strawberries in the sugar and cinnamon mixture until they are well coated. Chill in the refrigerator for at least 30 minutes.

When ready to serve, transfer the slices of panettone to a medium-hot grill. Grill the panettone for about 1 minute on each side or until golden brown.

Carefully remove the panettone from the grill and transfer to serving plates.

Top each slice of the panettone with mascarpone and the marinated strawberries. Serve immediately.

serves 6 | prep 30 mins + 6–8 hrs chilling/cooling | cook 20 mins

zucotto

Zucotto is a traditional Italian dessert that combines those natural partners, plain chocolate and black cherries.

INGREDIENTS
115 g/4 oz soft margarine, plus
   extra for greasing
100 g/3½ oz self-raising flour
2 tbsp cocoa powder
½ tsp baking powder
115 g/4 oz golden caster sugar
2 eggs, beaten
3 tbsp brandy
2 tbsp kirsch

filling
300 ml/10 fl oz double cream
25 g/1 oz icing sugar, sifted
55 g/2 oz toasted almonds, chopped
225 g/8 oz black cherries, stoned
55 g/2 oz plain chocolate,
   chopped finely

to decorate
1 tbsp cocoa powder
1 tbsp icing sugar
fresh cherries

VARIATION
If fresh cherries are not available, use drained canned cherries instead. Replace the kirsch with an almond-flavoured liqueur, such as amaretto.

Preheat the oven to 190°C/375°F/Gas Mark 5. Grease a 30 x 23-cm/12 x 9-inch swiss roll tin with margarine and line with baking paper. Sift the flour, cocoa powder and baking powder into a bowl. Add the sugar, margarine and eggs. Beat together until well mixed, then spoon into the prepared tin. Bake in the preheated oven for 15–20 minutes, or until well risen and firm to the touch. Leave to stand in the tin for 5 minutes, then turn out onto a wire rack.

Using the rim of a 1.2-litre/2-pint heatproof bowl as a guide, cut a circle from the cake and set aside. Line the bowl with clingfilm. Use the remaining cake, cutting it as necessary, to line the bowl. Place the brandy and kirsch in a small bowl and mix together. Sprinkle over the cake, including the reserved circle.

To make the filling, pour the cream into a separate bowl and add the icing sugar. Whip until thick, then fold in the almonds, cherries and chocolate. Fill the sponge mould with the cream mixture and press the cake circle on top. Cover with a plate and a weight and chill in the refrigerator for 6–8 hours, or overnight. When ready to serve, turn the zucotto out onto a serving plate. Decorate with cocoa powder and icing sugar, sifted over in alternating segments, and a few cherries.

makes 8 slices | prep 25 mins + 8 hrs chilling | cook 40 mins

sicilian cassata

This rich cake, with a filling of ricotta cheese, candied fruit, chopped nuts and chocolate, is a Sicilian specialty.

INGREDIENTS
175 g/6 oz butter, softened, plus extra for greasing
150 g/5½ oz self-raising flour
2 tbsp cocoa powder
1 tsp baking powder
175 g/6 oz golden caster sugar
3 eggs
icing sugar, for dusting
chocolate curls,* to decorate

filling
450 g/1 lb ricotta cheese
100 g/3½ oz plain chocolate, grated
85 g/3 oz golden caster sugar
3 tbsp Marsala
55 g/2 oz chopped candied peel
25 g/1 oz almonds, chopped

Preheat the oven to 190°C/375°F/Gas Mark 5. Grease and line the base of an 18-cm/7-inch round cake tin. Sift the flour, cocoa powder and baking powder into a large bowl. Add the butter, sugar and eggs and beat together until smooth and creamy. Pour the mixture into the tin and bake in the preheated oven for 30–40 minutes, until well risen and firm to the touch. Turn out onto a wire rack after 5 minutes to cool.

Wash and dry the cake tin and grease and line it again. To make the filling, rub the ricotta through a sieve into a bowl. Add the grated chocolate, sugar and Marsala and beat together thoroughly until the mixture is light and fluffy. Stir in the candied peel and almonds.

Cut the thin crust off the top of the cake and discard. Cut the cake horizontally into three layers. Place the first slice in the prepared tin and cover with half the ricotta mixture. Repeat the layers, finishing with a cake layer. Press down lightly, cover with a plate and a weight and chill in the refrigerator for 8 hours, or overnight. To serve, turn out the cake onto a serving plate. Dust with icing sugar and decorate with chocolate curls.

COOK'S TIP
*To make chocolate curls, spread a thin layer of melted chocolate onto a flat surface. Just when it appears to have set, but is still soft, hold a knife or scraper at a 45-degree angle to the surface and push it along to form long scrolls. As the curls form, lift them carefully with the point of a knife.

makes 12–14 slices | prep 25 mins | cook 1 hr

almond cake

This rich cake is delicious served with fruit as a dessert or simply with a cup of coffee for a mid-morning snack. Using potato flour is the secret of its wonderful, soft texture.

INGREDIENTS
butter, for greasing
3 eggs, separated
140 g/5 oz caster sugar
55 g/2 oz potato flour
140 g/5 oz almonds, blanched, peeled
    and finely chopped
finely grated rind of 1 orange
135 ml/4½ fl oz orange juice
salt
icing sugar, for dusting

Preheat the oven to 160°C/325°F/Gas Mark 3. Generously grease a round 20-cm/8-inch cake tin. Beat the egg yolks with the sugar in a medium bowl until pale and thick and the mixture leaves a ribbon trail when the whisk is lifted. Stir in the potato flour, almonds, orange rind and orange juice.

Whisk the egg whites with a pinch of salt in another bowl until stiff. Gently fold the whites into the egg yolk mixture.

Pour the mixture into the tin and bake in the preheated oven for 50–60 minutes, until golden and just firm to the touch. Turn out onto a wire rack. Sift over a little icing sugar before serving.

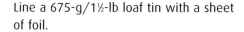

makes 16 slices | prep 1 hr 15 mins | cook 5 mins

rich chocolate loaf

*Another rich chocolate dessert, this loaf
is very simple to make and can be served
with coffee as well.*

INGREDIENTS
75 g/2¾ oz almonds
150 g/5½ oz plain chocolate
6 tbsp unsalted butter
210 g/7¼ oz canned condensed milk
2 tsp cinnamon
75 g/2¾ oz amaretti biscuits, broken
50 g/1¾ oz dried no-need-to-soak apricots,
   roughly chopped

Line a 675-g/1½-lb loaf tin with a sheet
of foil.

Using a sharp knife, roughly chop the
almonds into small pieces.

Place the chocolate, butter, milk and
cinnamon in a heavy-based saucepan.

Heat the chocolate mixture over a low heat
for 3–4 minutes, stirring with a wooden
spoon, or until the chocolate has melted.
Beat the mixture well.

Stir the almonds, biscuits and apricots
into the chocolate mixture, stirring with
a wooden spoon, until well mixed.

Pour the mixture into the prepared tin and
chill in the refrigerator for about 1 hour or
until set.

Cut the chocolate loaf into slices to serve.

makes 6 slices | prep 15 mins | cook 40 mins

pear & ginger cake

This deliciously buttery pear and ginger cake is ideal with coffee or you can serve it with cream for a delicious dessert.

INGREDIENTS
**200 g/7 oz unsalted butter, softened, plus
  extra for greasing
175 g/6 oz caster sugar
175 g/6 oz self-raising flour, sifted
3 tsp ginger
3 eggs, beaten
450 g/1 lb eating pears, peeled,
  cored and sliced thinly
1 tbsp demerara sugar
ice cream or cream, to serve**

Preheat the oven to 180°C/350°F/Gas Mark 4. Lightly grease a deep 20-cm/ 8-inch round cake tin and line the base with baking paper.

Using a whisk, combine 175 g/6 oz of the butter with the caster sugar, flour, ginger and eggs and mix to form a smooth consistency. Spoon into the prepared tin, levelling out the surface.

Arrange the pear slices over the cake mixture. Sprinkle with the demerara sugar and dot with the remaining butter.

Bake the cake in the preheated oven for 35–40 minutes, or until it is golden and feels springy to the touch.

Serve the pear and ginger cake warm, with ice cream.

makes 12–16 slices | prep 10 mins + 20 mins cooling | cook 40 mins

panforte di siena

Chewy, sticky panforte is the traditional Christmas cake of Siena. Chocolate was first added to the recipe when cocoa arrived from the New World and became the fashionable ingredient.

INGREDIENTS
butter, for greasing
55 g/2 oz candied cherries, cut into quarters
115 g/4 oz mixed candied orange and lemon peel, chopped finely
25 g/1 oz crystallized ginger, chopped coarsely
115 g/4 oz flaked almonds
115 g/4 oz hazelnuts, toasted and ground coarsely
55 g/2 oz plain flour
25 g/1 oz cocoa powder
1 tsp ground cinnamon
¼ tsp ground cloves
¼ tsp ground nutmeg
¼ tsp ground coriander
115 g/4 oz honey
115 g/4 oz golden caster sugar
1 tsp orange flower water
icing sugar, for dusting

VARIATION
You can replace the candied cherries with dried cranberries and the crystallized ginger with the same amount of candied pineapple.

Preheat the oven to 160°C/325°F/Gas Mark 3. Thoroughly grease the bottom of a 20-cm/8-inch loose-based cake or tart tin. Line the bottom with non-stick baking paper. Place the cherries, candied peel, ginger, almonds and hazelnuts in a medium-sized bowl. Sift in the flour, cocoa powder, cinnamon, cloves, nutmeg and coriander, and mix. Set aside.

Place the honey, sugar and orange flower water in a saucepan and heat gently until the sugar has dissolved. Bring the mixture to the boil and boil steadily until a temperature of 116°C/241°F has been reached on a sugar thermometer, or a small amount of the mixture forms a soft ball when dropped into cold water.

Quickly remove the pan from the heat and stir in the dry ingredients. Mix thoroughly and turn into the prepared tin. Spread evenly and bake in the preheated oven for 30 minutes. Leave to cool in the tin. Turn out and carefully peel away the lining paper. Dust icing sugar lightly over the top and cut into wedges to serve.

serves 10 | prep 15 mins + 8 hrs chilling | cook 5 mins

italian chocolate christmas pudding

This pudding is a wonderful alternative for anyone who dislikes a traditional Christmas pudding, but there is absolutely no reason why it should be served only at Christmas!

Grease an 850-ml/1½-pint heatproof bowl with butter. Place the candied fruit, raisins, orange rind and juice in a bowl and mix together. Put the single cream and chocolate in a pan and heat gently until the chocolate has melted. Stir until smooth, then stir in the fruit mixture. Let cool.

Place the cream cheese and a little of the chocolate mixture in a large bowl and beat together until smooth, then stir in the remaining chocolate mixture. Stir in the broken amaretti biscuits. Pour into the prepared bowl, cover with clingfilm and chill in the refrigerator overnight.

To serve, turn the pudding out onto a chilled serving plate. Pour the whipping cream into a bowl and add the amaretto. Whip lightly until slightly thickened. Pour some of the cream over the pudding and sprinkle grated chocolate over the top. Serve with the remaining cream.

VARIATION
For a change, substitute the amaretti biscuits with crushed ginger nuts and replace the amaretto with the same quantity of brandy.

INGREDIENTS
butter, for greasing
115 g/4 oz mixed candied fruit, chopped
55 g/2 oz raisins
grated rind of ½ orange
3 tbsp orange juice
3 tbsp single cream
350 g/12 oz plain chocolate, chopped
115 g/ 4 oz cream cheese
115 g/4 oz amaretti biscuits, broken into
  coarse pieces

to serve
125 ml/4 fl oz whipping cream
2 tbsp amaretto
25 g/1 oz plain chocolate, grated

serves 6 | prep 20 mins | cook 0 mins

ricotta ice cream

The ricotta cheese adds a creamy flavour, while the nuts add a crunchy texture to this ice cream, which needs to be chilled in the freezer overnight.

INGREDIENTS
25 g/1 oz pistachio nuts
25 g/1 oz walnuts or pecan nuts
25 g/1 oz toasted chopped hazelnuts
grated rind of 1 orange
grated rind of 1 lemon
25 g/1 oz crystallized or preserved ginger
25 g/1 oz candied cherries
25 g/1 oz dried apricots
25 g/1 oz raisins
500 g/1lb 2 oz ricotta cheese
2 tbsp maraschino, amaretto or brandy
1 tsp vanilla essence
4 egg yolks
125 g/4½ oz caster sugar

to decorate
whipped cream
a few candied cherries, pistachio nuts
   or mint leaves

Roughly chop the pistachio nuts and walnuts and mix with the toasted hazelnuts and the orange and lemon rind.

Finely chop the ginger, cherries, apricots and raisins, and add to the bowl.

Stir the ricotta cheese evenly through the fruit mixture, then beat in the liqueur and vanilla essence.

Put the egg yolks and sugar in a bowl and whisk hard until very thick and creamy – they may be whisked over a saucepan of gently simmering water to speed up the process. Leave to cool if necessary.

Carefully fold the ricotta mixture evenly through the beaten eggs and sugar until smoothly blended.

Line a 18 x 12-cm/7 x 5-inch loaf tin with a double layer of clingfilm. Pour in the ricotta mixture, level the top, cover with more clingfilm and chill in the freezer until firm – at least overnight.

To serve, carefully remove the ice-cream from the tin and peel off the paper. Place on a serving dish and decorate with whipped cream, candied cherries, pistachio nuts and/or mint leaves. Serve in slices.

serves 4 | prep 15 mins + 5 hrs freezing | cook 6 mins

lemon granita

A delightful end to a meal or a refreshing way to cleanse the palate, granitas are made from slushy ice, so they need to be served very quickly.

INGREDIENTS
3 lemons
175 ml/6 fl oz lemon juice
100 g/3½ oz caster sugar
600 ml/1 pint cold water

To make lemon granita, finely grate the lemon rind.

Place the lemon rind, lemon juice, and caster sugar in a saucepan. Bring the mixture to the boil and simmer for 5-6 minutes or until thick and syrupy. Leave to cool.

Once cooled, stir in the cold water and pour into a shallow freezer container with a lid.

Freeze the granita for 4–5 hours, stirring occasionally to break up the ice. Serve as a dessert or as a palate cleanser between courses.

VARIATION
To make coffee granita, place 2 tbsp instant coffee and 2 tbsp sugar in a bowl and pour over 2 tbsp hot water, stirring until dissolved. Stir in 600 ml/ 1 pint cold water and 2 tbsp rum or brandy. Pour the mixture into a shallow freezer container with a lid. Freeze for at least 6 hours, stirring occasionally, to create a grainy texture.

serves 4 | prep 10 mins + 1 hr chilling | cook 20 mins

marsala cherries

This is a popular Venetian dish, made with Morello cherries – the variety most widely grown in Italy.

INGREDIENTS
140 g/5 oz caster sugar
thinly pared rind of 1 lemon
5-cm/2-inch piece of cinnamon stick
1 cup water
1 cup Marsala
900 g/2 lb Morello cherries, stoned
150 ml/5 fl oz double cream

Put the sugar, lemon rind, cinnamon stick, water and Marsala in a heavy-based saucepan and bring to the boil, stirring constantly. Reduce the heat and simmer for 5 minutes. Remove the cinnamon stick.

Add the cherries, cover and simmer gently for 10 minutes. Using a slotted spoon, transfer the cherries to a bowl.

Return the saucepan to the heat and bring to the boil over a high heat. Boil for 3–4 minutes, until thick and syrupy. Pour the syrup over the cherries and set aside to cool, then chill for at least 1 hour.

Whisk the cream until stiff peaks form. Divide the cherries and syrup between four individual dishes or glasses, top with the cream and serve.

VARIATION
Substitute a full-bodied red wine for the Marsala.

makes 40 | prep 20 mins | cook 20 mins

mini florentines

Serve these biscuits at the end of a meal with coffee, or arrange in a shallow presentation box for an attractive gift.

INGREDIENTS
75 g/2¾ oz butter
75 g/2¾ oz caster sugar
25 g/1 oz sultanas or raisins
25 g/1 oz candied cherries, chopped
25 g/1 oz crystallized ginger, chopped
25 g/1 oz sunflower seeds
100 g/3½ oz flaked almonds
2 tbsp double cream
175 g/6 oz plain chocolate

Preheat the oven to 180°C/350°F/Gas Mark 4. Grease and flour two baking sheets and line with baking paper.

Place the butter in a small saucepan and heat gently until melted. Add the sugar, stir until dissolved, then bring the mixture to the boil. Remove from the heat and stir in the sultanas or raisins, cherries, ginger, sunflower seeds and almonds. Mix well, then beat in the cream.

Place small teaspoons of the fruit and nut mixture on the prepared baking tray, allowing plenty of space for the mixture to spread. Bake in the preheated oven for 10–12 minutes, or until light golden in colour.

Remove from the oven and, while still hot, use a circular biscuit cutter to pull in the edges to form a perfect circle.

Leave to cool and crispen before removing from the baking sheet.

Melt most of the chocolate and spread it on a sheet of baking paper. When the chocolate is on the point of setting, place the biscuits flat-side down on the chocolate and leave to harden completely.

Cut around the florentines and remove from the baking paper. Spread a little more chocolate on the coated side of the florentines and use a fork to mark waves in the chocolate. Leave to set. Arrange the florentines on a plate (or in a presentation box for a gift) with alternate sides facing upwards. Keep cool.

makes 16 | prep 20 mins | cook 40 mins

chocolate biscotti

These dry biscuits are delicious served with black coffee or dessert wine after your evening meal.

INGREDIENTS
oil, for greasing
1 egg
150 g/5½ oz caster sugar
1 tsp vanilla essence
125 g/4½ oz flour
½ tsp baking powder
1 tsp ground cinnamon
50 g/1¾ oz plain chocolate, chopped roughly
50 g/1¾ oz toasted flaked almonds
50 g/1¾ oz pine kernels

Preheat the oven to 180°C/350°F/Gas Mark 4. Lightly grease a large baking sheet.

Whisk the egg, sugar and vanilla extract in a mixing bowl with an electric mixer until it is thick and pale – ribbons of mixture should trail from the whisk as you lift it.

Sift the flour, baking powder and cinnamon into a separate bowl, then sift into the egg mixture and fold in gently. Stir in the chocolate, almonds and pine kernels.

Turn on to a lightly floured work surface and shape into a flat log, 23 cm/9 inches long and 2 cm/¾ inch wide. Transfer the log to the prepared baking sheet.

Bake in the preheated oven for 20–25 minutes or until golden. Remove from the oven and leave to cool for 5 minutes or until firm.

Transfer the log to a cutting board. Using a serrated bread knife, cut the log on the diagonal into slices about 1 cm/ ½ inch thick and arrange them on the baking sheet. Cook for 10–15 minutes, turning halfway through the cooking time.

Leave to cool for about 5 minutes, then transfer to a wire rack to cool completely.

makes 24 | prep 20 mins | cook 15 mins

white chocolate florentines

These attractive jewelled biscuits are coated with white chocolate to give them a delicious flavour.

INGREDIENTS
200 g/7 oz butter
225 g/8 oz caster sugar
125 g/4½ oz walnuts, chopped
125 g/4½ oz almonds, chopped
55 g/2 oz sultanas, chopped
25 g/1 oz candied cherries,
25 g/1 oz mixed candied peel,
   chopped finely
2 tbsp single cream
225 g/8 oz white chocolate

Preheat the oven to 180°C/350°F/Gas Mark 4. Line three to four baking sheets with baking paper.

Put the butter into a saucepan and melt over a low heat and then add the sugar, stirring until it has dissolved. Boil the mixture for exactly 1 minute. Remove from the heat.

Add the walnuts, almonds, sultanas, cherries, peel and cream to the pan, stirring well to mix.

Drop heaped teaspoonfuls of the mixture onto the baking sheets, allowing plenty of room for the biscuits to spread while cooking. Bake in the preheated oven for 10 minutes, or until golden brown.

Remove the biscuits from the oven and neaten the edges with a knife while they are still warm. Leave to cool slightly, then transfer to a wire rack to cool completely.

Melt the chocolate in a heatproof bowl placed over a saucepan of gently simmering water. Spread the underside of the biscuits with chocolate and use a fork to make wavy lines across the surface. Leave to cool completely.

Store in an airtight tin in a cool place.

makes 20 | prep 5 mins + 1 hr chilling | cook 5 mins

italian chocolate truffles

These are flavoured with almonds and chocolate, and are simplicity itself to make. Served with coffee, they are the perfect end to a meal.

INGREDIENTS
175 g/6 oz plain chocolate
2 tbsp amaretto or
    orange-flavoured liqueur
40 g/1½ oz unsalted butter
50 g/1¾ oz icing sugar
50 g/1¾ oz ground almonds
50 g/1¾ oz grated milk chocolate

Melt the chocolate with the liqueur in a heatproof bowl set over a saucepan of hot water, stirring until well combined.

Add the butter and stir until it has melted. Stir in the icing sugar and the ground almonds.

Leave the mixture in a cool place until firm enough to roll into 24 balls.

Place the grated chocolate on a plate and roll the truffles in the chocolate to coat them.

Place the truffles in paper sweet cases and chill for at least 1 hour.